Staying One, Remaining Open

Educating Leaders for a 21st-Century Church

Richard J. Jones and J. Barney Hawkins IV, eds.

Morehouse Publishing

NEW YORK · HARRISBURG · DENVER

Unless otherwise noted, the Scripture quotations contained herein are from the New Revised Standard Version Bible, copyright © 1989 by the Division of Christian Education of the National Council of Churches of Christ in the U.S.A. Used by permission. All rights reserved.

A version of the chapter "Don't Forget to Remember: Identity in Deuteronomy and Ruth" by Judy Fentress Williams will appear in *Teaching Our Story: Narrative Leadership and Pastoral Formation,* edited by Lawrence A. Golemon (Herndon, Va.: Alban Institute, 2009). Used by permission.

Morehouse Publishing, 4775 Linglestown Road, Harrisburg, PA 17112

Morehouse Publishing, 445 Fifth Avenue, New York, NY 10016

Morehouse Publishing is an imprint of Church Publishing Incorporated.

Cover art courtesy of Virginia Theological Seminary

Cover design by Christina Moore

Typeset by MediaLynx

Library of Congress Cataloging-in-Publication Data

Staying one, remaining open: educating leaders for a 21st-century church / Richard J. Jones, J. Barney Hawkins IV, editors.
  p. cm.
 Includes bibliographical references.
 ISBN 978-0-8192-2396-8 (pbk.)
1. Mission of the church. 2. Multiculturalism—Religious aspects—Christianity. 3. Church. 4. Anglican Communion. I. Jones, Richard J. II. Hawkins, J. Barney (James Barney)
 BV601.8.S73 2009
 262'.037308—dc22

  2009046693

Printed in the United States of America

10 11 12 13 14 15   10 9 8 7 6 5 4 3 2

Contents

Foreword

The tenure of the Very Rev. Martha Horne as dean and president of the Virginia Theological Seminary (1993–2007) coincided with a period of dynamic theological contention in the Christian family worldwide and in the Anglican Communion in particular.

It was also a time of major transition in the life of Virginia Seminary itself. Distinguished long-term professors retired in the late 1980s and early 1990s, and Dean Horne recruited a lively faculty reflective of the diversity of the church.

These essays in her honor celebrate the diversity of the Seminary and give evidence of the gracious, welcoming climate over which Dean Horne presided during her tenure. In her person and in her leadership, she witnessed to the hospitality of the Gospel of Jesus Christ in its welcome to all sorts and conditions of folk.

Current biblical scholarship is increasingly aware of the different, even competing, claims in both the Hebrew Scriptures and the New Testament. Martha Horne's leadership of a faithful community of scholars contributed to a climate where the promise of the Acts of the Apostles might be fulfilled, that all may hear in their own tongues the marvelous things that God has done.

This collection of essays honors the faith and hospitality that Dean Horne embodies.

The Rt. Rev. Peter James Lee
Bishop of Virginia
Chairman of the Board of Trustees
of Virginia Theological Seminary, 1993–2009

Editors' Introduction

When the Very Rev. Ian S. Markham became the dean and president of Virginia Theological Seminary in 2007, he suggested a collection of essays to honor the deanship of his predecessor, the Very Rev. Martha J. Horne. Faculty members who served during Dean Horne's tenure were invited to reflect on the challenge of living with difference, staying one and remaining open. As in most seminaries where women and men are being shaped for leadership in the Church, Virginia Seminary's faculty is not of one mind about the important questions of the day. In his afterword, Dean Markham asks the question that is always with us: how far can disagreement extend in a seminary community?

Dean Horne lived into the challenges of her time, even as she cherished the Seminary's rich past. She practiced the art of conversation with trustees, faculty, staff, students, and alumni/ae. She listened well and patiently. In countless faculty meetings she took account of deep-rooted and ongoing disagreements in matters of faith and practice. She presided over a faculty that lived with a divided mind—yet remained one in commitment to the Seminary's mission. Virginia Theological Seminary continues to shape faithful leaders who understand the necessity for Christ's Church to remain one.

The Horne years were characterized by an appreciation of Anglicanism as a historic and lively branch of Christendom that should be treasured as a gift for the whole Church. Dean Horne was always sensitive to the larger context in which the Episcopal Church and the Seminary find themselves, in the company of sister denominations and in the wider Anglican Communion. Out of her personal experience and careful exegesis of Holy Scripture, Dean Horne embraced diversity and practiced an inclusivity in matters of gender, race, and ethnicity that was biblically grounded and pastorally informed. The essays which follow display a colorful palette of theological convictions that mirror her intellectual curiosity and the issues current in her time as dean.

These essays are windows into the theological pluralism of a seminary faculty where learning and living go hand in hand with diversity, division, protracted discussions and lasting disagreements. Virginia Seminary is a Christian community that practices conversation, cherishes scripture and tradition, and values the unity which is ours in Jesus Christ. The practice of staying open and remaining one is the faithful witness of one community of Christian scholars in these challenging days of a new century.

We live with disagreement and division as we discuss God's mission in a world shaken by the clash of cultural and religious identities. The ways and means of our worship and prayer life provoke long debates and reveal the divisions among us. We wrestle with the biblical texts we interpret and preach. We often stand in different places.

Read these essays and hear the voices of a Christian community which works to stay open and to remain one.

Richard J. Jones and *J. Barney Hawkins IV*

Diversity and
Christian Identity

Allan M. Parrent

> Now I appeal to you, brothers and sisters, by the
> name of our Lord Jesus Christ, that all of you be in
> agreement and that there be no divisions among
> you, but that you be united in the same mind and
> the same purpose. For it has been reported to me
> by Chloe's people that there are quarrels among
> you [my brothers and sisters]. What I mean is that
> each one of you says, "I belong to Paul," or "I belong
> to Apollos," or "I belong to Cephas," or "I belong to
> Christ." (1 Corinthians 1:10–12)

So, we might ask, what else is new? So there are quarrels
or divisions within the Church. There have always been
divisions in the Church. There will always be divisions
in the Church. The same is true of the political and
social life of this country and I daresay of every country. There
are divisions within even the human community and institution made up of Adam's sons and daughters.

And is that after all such a bad thing? Do we really prefer a stifling conformity to the rich creativity of human diversity? Indeed, precisely because we are Adam's sons and daughters, to whom might we be willing to entrust the determination of what is to be conformed to, and the power to enforce it? And what is wrong with Paul, Apollos, and Cephas anyway? They are, after all, as Paul later informs us, servants through whom many came to believe. And a diversity or pluralism of religious approaches, or theological emphases, or expected norms of moral behavior can in fact attract different people and even swell the roster of communicants.

But on the other hand (a phrase that any good Niebuhrian will always interject at some point), there are clearly limits to diversity within any community that is concerned about maintaining its integrity, its coherence, and a clear sense of its identity. At some point a group or community or institution will be forced to clarify its identity, to proclaim its distinctiveness, to set limits beyond which it can no longer conscientiously accept further diversity.

One of the purposes of the Inter-Anglican Theological and Doctrinal Commission (meeting at this seminary as of the writing of this chapter) is to seek to define with some specificity Anglican identity, Anglican distinctiveness, the theological integrity of Anglicanism. In an earlier document the Commission, noting the danger for a church that has consciously attempted to embrace pluralism, said: "For too long Anglicans have appeared willing to evade responsible theological reflection and dialogue by acquiescing automatically and immediately in the coexistence of incompatible views, opinion and policies."

Anglicans are of course not alone in raising the questions of identity. A recently concluded four year self-study of the United Methodist Church found that one of the most serious problems for United Methodism was the perception that there are no theological norms beyond which it is impossible to go and still be a Methodist.

It seems that today we are experiencing in both the Church and in the broader society two conflicting pressures or movements. One is toward greater diversity, pluralism, and multiculturalism, manifestations of which are to be accepted and incorporated within the inclusive arms of the Church or the culture. The other pressure is toward distinctiveness, particularity, identity, and the drawing of lines in the name of theological or cultural integrity that may of necessity exclude. As Christians we are called to be agents of reconciliation, but also not to be tossed about by every wind of doctrine. We are warned about being judgmental, but also about not calling evil good and good evil. The fact of the matter is, of course, that each pressure or movement has its own validity, within limits, and each can offer a corrective vision to and for the other. Conversely, each has its own dangers, dangers that will surely be realized if each does not have the other to keep it within necessary bounds.

The Dangers of Each

George Kennan once wrote, in a different context, that any idea carried to its logical extreme becomes a caricature of itself. That is certainly true of these conflicting movements as we experience them within the Church and in our culture. Reinhold Niebuhr was constantly alerting us to the dangers of both Scylla and Charybdis, those two hazards of Greek mythology on either side of the Straits of Messina and endangered ships that veered too far to one side in order to avoid the danger on the other side. He used the imagery in seeking to maintain the ever-shifting balance in political ethics between freedom and order, or liberty and equality, and to avoid both the Scylla of anarchy and the Charybdis of tyranny. The same warning is important in dealing with the pressures for greater diversity, pluralism, or multiculturalism on one hand and for maintaining distinctiveness, particularity, or identity on the other.

When diversity is elevated to the role of a first principle, as in some parts of academia today, there is little room then left for maintaining a distinctive identity or cultural or moral norms that someone might find offensive. One result is moral relativism, for who are we to say that one sub-group is right or wrong? Another result is a litany of "isms"—oppressive devices of which anyone is guilty who is so perceived, or who makes truth claims that would give priority within the larger community to one vision of truth over others. The opposition to such perceived exclusiveness can get humorous at times, such as the demand on one college campus for unisex bathrooms on the grounds that having different bathrooms for the sexes was akin to having separate drinking fountains for the races.

But equally, when the emphasis on the distinctiveness and particularity of group identity becomes excessive, it can devolve into a new tribalism, into theological or political or cultural balkanization. At that point, as one wag put it, "groups are us." People come to identify almost exclusively with their own race, gender, ethnic group, lifestyle enclave, interest group, or sect, to the virtual exclusion of common commitments and allegiances to more inclusive communities.

In politics I need only to mention places like Bosnia, the Sudan, Sri Lanka, Rwanda, and to a lesser degree Quebec, where tribalism seems to be reasserting itself. In education we are aware of the denigration in some places of any larger universal human intellectual tradition, and the belief that the purpose of education is ideological brainwashing.

In philosophy, "perspectivism" has become popular in recent years, the view that there is no objectivity, there is only solidarity with those who share the same perspective, or the same "story," as we, as if we were totally culturally conditioned all the way down and unable to transcend our historical context. Theologian Carl Braaten, among others, is concerned about religious thinkers who "are surrendering to a neo-tribalism in which some distinguishing mark of identity—gender, color, class or ideology—dominates the entire theological spectrum."[1]

The Necessity of Each

But in spite of these dangers, both of these movements are fundamentally important for the life and health of both the Christian community and the broader community. In the search for inclusivity, some emphasize the need for greater diversity and pluralism, and properly so. In the search for identity, others emphasize the need for greater clarity about distinctiveness and particularity, and properly so. One legitimately asks, "Are we too narrowly exclusive? Should we be more open to other perspectives and life experiences?" The other legitimately asks, "Do we stand for anything distinctive? What is our identity?"

Paul's appeal in our text to "have no divisions among you," and to be united as Christians "in the same mind and the same purpose," is in part a call to inclusivity. There may well be distinctions among the Paulists, the Apolloists, and the Cephasists, but let us focus rather on that which transcends our quarrels and our divisions and unites us. Christ is not divided. At the same time, however, that same appeal from Paul is an appeal for clarity about identity. We are to be united, not just for the sake of unity, but in order to be united in the same mind as Jesus Christ and for his purposes. That is distinctive.

So, not unlike our larger contemporary society, the church has a Scylla and Charybdis problem. One shoal is hyperpluralism or multiculturalism, diversity for the sake of diversity, and a surface unity made possible only at the expense of the social and moral ecology of our common life, something that is threatened today at least as much as the ecology of the natural world. The other shoal is tribalism, polarization, and exclusivity made possible only by group self-absorption and a false sense of superiority.

Unity and Identity in Baptism

How might the Christian community maintain what is essential in both of these movements, while avoiding the destructive shoals that loom on either side of our passageway toward faithful and responsible Christian living? The beginnings of an answer may lie in Paul's reference in our text to baptism, and to the identity of the one in whose name all are baptized, the Lord, Jesus Christ. That baptismal unity makes rather unimportant the diverse persons who performed our baptisms, be they Paul, Apollos, or Cephas. And it certainly makes it all the more wrong to appeal to that symbol of Christian unity, baptism, to justify factions. Just as Christians do not define ourselves by who baptized us, so we do not define ourselves fundamentally by race, gender, ethnicity, or interest group. We are defined rather by our union with Christ in baptism and our participation, with a diversity of Christian brothers and sisters, in the body of Christ. That baptismal unity is indeed the source of our identity, our distinctiveness.

But Paul's appeal for unity in mind and purpose is not referring to just any old mind and purpose, so long as they are broad enough to encompass the diversity of all possible factions. Rather it is a call for unity through conformity, not with this world, but with the mind of Christ and his purposes. And that can be exclusive. That can set limits on diversity. That can mean reminding ourselves, as did Luther when he faced temptations, "I have been baptized." That is, we have a particular identity that sets some boundaries, boundaries that are set, paradoxically, for the sake of real Christian freedom.

C.S. Lewis once observed that "If all experienced God in the same way and returned him an identical worship, the song of the church triumphant would have no symphony; it would be like an orchestra in which all the instruments played the same note." Gilbert Meilander, who is Professor of Christian Ethics at Valparaiso University, says that that image from Lewis gives a transcendent ground to our affirmations of diversity. But, he continues, it does not invite a flaccid relativism which supposes that it is just fine to want to play in this symphony while constantly hitting wrong notes, or I might add, using an entirely different score. The image is grounded fundamentally not in a commitment to individual diversity, but in commitment to, and love for, what is ultimately true and good. If our commitment to diversity is grounded only in individual self-expression, without regard for that more ultimate truth and goodness against which its divergence is measured, it will only lead to further disarray.

Paul's word to the church in Corinth, then, is a word for the Church in every place and time: "I appeal to you, brothers and sisters, by the name of our Lord Jesus Christ, that all of you be in agreement and that there be no divisions among you, but that you be united in the same mind and the same purpose."

Note

1   Carl Braaten, in Wolfhart Pannenberg, *An Introduction to Systematic Theology* (Grand Rapids, MI: Wm. B. Eerdmans, 1991), jacket.

Diversity and
the Tea Lady

Richard J. Jones

C an we still keep her on? She sees to it there is tea on hand, cups and saucers washed, and old newspapers and stray staples put in the trash. But the tea lady belongs to a past way of living. If she goes, who looks after the common room to keep it attractive? Today's drive for cultural and ethnic diversity in American social institutions threatens to leave the house with no tended common space. Under a rule of self-service, with no host, who makes welcome?[1]

Christians in the United States partake with others this year in a season of elevated self-consciousness about our society. We discuss the relations between subcultures and the general culture in which all share. A presidential election evokes incessant calculating and speculating about the black vote, the Hispanic vote, women's votes, and the white- and blue-collar votes. Voting behavior is observed to vary between the constellations of our several subcultures. Yet subcultures' voting behavior is evoked and guided by the ideas, the legal sanctions, and the physical communication devices and vote-tallying products characteristic of the general culture.

The meshing of subcultures within general American culture reminds me of the meshing of gear wheels in a drive mechanism. Some wheels are large, some very small; some rotate in one plane and some in another; sometimes the wheels are engaged with one another, sometimes they do not touch. I want to ask how the Holy Spirit—God at work among us, even now—might be working in our day to clean, lubricate, or reconfigure these wheels. Could the tea lady still be visited by the Holy Spirit?

Groups and Their Cultures

When I speak of "culture," I follow the Mennonite anthropologist Paul G. Hiebert, who spent much of his life in south India but taught in Seattle and Chicago. In his 1976 textbook *Cultural Anthropology,* Hiebert recognized that "human beings are biological, psychological, social, economic, political, religious and historical beings—and even more." Hence he proposed a very broad definition of human culture: *"the integrated system of learned patterns of behavior, ideas, and products characteristic of a society."* [2]

I find each element of Hiebert's definition helpful as I seek to discover my part in the unfinished, cultural-boundary-crossing mission of God's Church in this world, and as I encourage others to play their parts.

The first element calls attention to *patterns.* There is of course change and chance in human life, but to the observant there also appear repeating patterns. Empirical scientists seek these patterns. Artists detect these patterns.

Reviewing a recent English translation of Leo Tolstoy's *War and Peace,* James Wood observes how the vividly rendered characters are also, in their creator's eyes, types. Tolstoy ponders and plays with the simultaneous truths of individual unique-ness *and* involuntary similarity.

> The old prince, ignoring his son Andrei's efforts
> to tell him about Napoleon's designs, breaks into
> creaky song and sings "in an old man's off-key voice."
> A few pages later, we see "the old prince in his old
> man's spectacles and his white smock." An old man
> with an old man's voice and old man's spectacles:
> Tolstoy pushes such characterization towards the
> simplest tautology: What was the old man like?
> He was like an old man—that is to say, like all old
> men. What is a young man like? He is like a young
> man—that is to say, like all young men. What is a
> happy young man like? Like all happy young men.
> The Austrian minister of war is described thus:
> "He had an intelligent and characteristic head." A
> character will tend to look characteristic in both
> senses of the word: full of character, and somehow
> typical.

A good student of culture, like a good novelist, cannot be content with cherished smells and flashes of memory, with par-ticularities and captivating uniqueness. A good understanding prizes all these, yet also notices patterns. Hiebert notes that the patterns build on one another. They combine to form recogniz-able, orderly, predictable structures. The patterns, if one can ever succeed in taking them all in and mapping them, form an *integrated system.*

These patterns, occurring within an integrated system and helping to sustain it, are not the inventions of one individual, or of one generation. Nor are they innate. Biological processes are innate, but cultural patterns are *learned*. We respond to our social environment, just as our bodies respond to our natural environment. We adapt to what is offered to us. We respond to stimuli. We imitate our mother's speech, just as we suck her milk and take as food what she dishes out. We imitate our par-ents, elders, and coevals. We make their ways ours. Patterns can of course be unlearned, and thus are cultures changed. But to mature as a social being is first to learn your mother tongue—and everything else your mother has to offer.

Hiebert distinguishes three realms in which our culture offers us patterns: patterns of *ideas*, patterns of *behavior*, and patterns for making *physical objects*. If we liked, we might speak of mental culture, behavioral culture, and physical culture. Because these patterns are linked, each of the three realms affects and is affected by the other two.

Take the ashtray—if you can still locate one! In my boyhood that artifact occupied quite a few cupboards and tabletops. Heavy glass ashtrays carried advertisements. Elegant Chinese cloisonné ashtrays delighted the eye. Pedestal ashtrays spared the carpets in hotel lobbies. These artifacts both responded to and encouraged patterns of cigar- and cigarette-smoking behavior—learned from movies in the 1920s, then unlearned through Surgeon Generals' warnings and court-ordered negative advertising in the 1970s. Linked to both material smoking paraphernalia and observable smoking behavior were ideas—first the idea that smoking is soothing or sophisticated, later the unsettling idea that smoking is dangerous or disgusting.

So it seems plausible to me to view culture as an integrated system of learned patterns of behavior, ideas, and artifacts characteristic of a society. This last element of Hiebert's definition embeds culture in a *society*.

"Society" is a demographic notion. You can take a census of a society, film its members in action, map its territory, and reconstruct its rise and demise. Culture, on the other hand, cannot be grasped by observation alone. This is because culture exists in the mind as well as outwardly. Culture is ideas as well as behavior and objects. We do well to speak carefully and not treat "culture" and "society" as interchangeable. Where there is no society, there will of course be no culture. Yet the two notions are distinct. Conceivably a society might remain unchanged in location, size, wealth, religion, and language, yet experience rapid change in key values, role definitions, institutions, and behaviors. We could say this society is experiencing cultural change. By the same token, one can conceive of a diaspora in which members of a society are forced to migrate. They manage to regroup in some alien spot on the earth, altered in their shared status, wealth, and numbers, yet within their society preserving their culture intact. Indeed, a culture can sometimes be renewed and strengthened when a society resists a serious effort by outside enemies to kill it off.

So a society is not the same thing as a culture, yet every society, small or large, has a culture. On this view, religion is an aspect of culture, just as language is an aspect of culture. Culture comprises language, religion, and the many media available for us to express our ever-so-plastic humanity. Like Tolstoy's Austrian minister of war with his characteristic head, so our society, and every society, has its characteristic culture. That culture, meshing with our individual personalities, shapes us into the broadly predictable sort of social human beings we are.

Subcultural Differences and Cultural Change

What is a society? I conceive of a society simply as a very large human group. This large group in turn is made up of subgroups. If the general society shares one general culture, so its subgroups have their own subcultures. In this manner of speaking, the prefix "sub-" does not signify lesser or inferior. A subculture is simply a component of the larger, more generally shared culture.

A society's subgroups may be based on kinship, or they may be based, in the words of Franklin Giddings, on some "consciousness of kind."[3] Subgroups may be ephemeral or highly institutionalized and long-lasting. They may be bound together by location—we of this neighborhood, we of these Appalachian Mountains. Groups may be bound together by a shared interest or capacity, and that capacity may either be achieved by effort or ascribed by others without need for effort. If a whole society is characterized by a shared and characteristic culture, so is each subgroup characterized by its own subculture.

On the map of American society which I learned while acquiring my version of American culture, I see American subcultures as distinct zones. These zones are demarcated and labeled according to such anthropological theory as I have imbibed. My mental map includes farming, academic, and ecclesiastical subcultures, to name just the ones I have participated in directly. My map also recognizes the African-American, Hispanic, and Appalachian subcultures. Some subcultures are shared with societies outside the population of the United States. Hispanic culture is shared with Latin America, francophone culture with Quebec and New Brunswick, and African-American culture to varying degrees with the African diaspora in the Caribbean and the cultures of societies remaining on the African continent. Appalachian culture has historic roots in Great Britain, spreading over time to urban areas including Washington, Cincinnati, Nashville, and Chicago, yet its home territory remains the Appalachian Mountains.

Subcultures have complex relations with the general culture. They share many of the traits of the general culture. Appalachian people, African-American people, Hispanic Americans, and academics all drive on the right. All drink Coca-Cola. Other traits of the general culture, however, they may not share—or each may share a different range of that culture.

Subcultures have their own distinct configuration. They have distinctive centers of meaning or points of density. In such zones, participants in the subcultures demonstrate that some clustering of ideas, behavior, and products holds particular importance for them. Thus Mardi Gras forms a larger center of meaning in the subculture of New Orleans and Mobile than in general American culture. Some subcultures will participate in the general culture in all areas except dress, or all areas except women's dress. Other subcultures will participate in the general culture only in matters compelled by law. Some subcultures will distinguish themselves by the language or dialect spoken among members; others by their religious practices; still others by products, such as medicines or music, which are important to them but unknown or disapproved of in the general culture.

Over time, the population shares of subgroups in American society change, according to birth rates, death rates, and net immigration. Just now the Hispanic subgroup in the population is increasing its demographic share, as well as its status. In our present moment of elevated cultural self-consciousness, efforts to accelerate assimilation are met with calls to preserve difference. My parish offers free English classes under the name "New Neighbors," and the American Civil Liberties Union demands that local and national government treat illegal immigrants more generously. At the same time, school principals, city recreation departments, and churches have to accommodate the desire of subgroups to play a part. Will the wheels of these subcultures mesh?

"Live separately and let live" has at times been the plea of the Amish, the Fundamental Latter-Day Saints, the Pueblo, the International Society of Krishna Consciousness, and the Nation of Islam. Separation remains the goal of a strong group in Quebec, as of those in many societies who fight to liberate their group from demeaning or exploitative relationships.

The Canadian philosopher and politician Charles Taylor has helped me understand the current widespread conviction that "the withholding of recognition can be a form of oppression. . . . Within these perspectives," Taylor says, "misrecognition shows not just a lack of due respect. It can inflict a grievous wound, saddling its victims with a crippling self-hatred. [On this understanding,] due recognition is not just a courtesy we owe people. It is a vital human need." [4]

Tea lady, take note whom you recognize, and how. Even

though they move the furniture around and use unfamiliar brews, these subgroups require your welcome.

Most American subgroups seem to desire to be recognized with respect by other groups, rather than to sever all relations with other groups, however alien. Market forces are too strong, and the desire to participate in wealth accumulation and upward social mobility is too keen for separation. Love of soccer—like the love of rugby two decades ago in South Africa—erodes barriers. When it comes to subgroups within the Episcopal Church of the United States, and other Christian bodies, we are further constrained from separation by a horror of tearing apart the Body of Christ.

So we will continue the work of welcome. American subcultures will offer degrees of recognition to other subcultures where recognition is due, as they are able to give, and as the other is able to receive.

What do Christians, shaped as they are by their general culture and specific subcultures, bring to this work of welcome? For one thing, we recognize each person as made in the image of God, proved worthy of our recognition by Christ's willingness to die on behalf of all, and fit to become a dwelling place of the Holy Spirit. It is a different thing, however, to pronounce as approved and blessed by God all the ideas, behaviors, and products of a person's culture—that inherited medium through which persons express their humanity and construct their lives in community, collaborating with the Holy Spirit. For there is that within each of us, and within our culture, which resists the Holy Spirit. Reinhold Niebuhr long ago persuaded me to believe in both moral man and immoral society.

To declare all human culture, including the general American culture and every identifiable subculture participating in general American culture, to be approved and blessed by God is more than I can do. Our general American culture is the operating system of a social structure and of social mechanisms which help produce both happy, whole people *and* deformed, corrupt people. Most of us happy ones receive without qualms the deference, protection, and comforts which the general culture assures to people in my social position. There is much in the general American culture, and in the culture of my particular privileged and dominant WASP subgroup, to repent of. I have personal sins to confess—of sloth and resistance to the Holy Spirit, of greed and indifference, of routinely not loving my neighbor as myself. Likewise my group, the dominant class and ethnic group in American society, has much pride, blindness, and bullying to repent of.

If my culture can resist the Holy Spirit, I have to suspect the same may occur for other cultures. In every society, the culture nurtures, presses upon, and shapes individuals. At the same time, individuals make choices, generate new ideas, behaviors, and products, and so contribute to cultural change, and to social change. In this push and pull between culture and the person, and between the inherited and the yet to be, particular institutions play their parts. A theological seminary is a small player to hope to influence general American culture, compared with large primary and secondary school systems, or with universities, or with the economic and legal power of foundations and governments. Yet it matters that even the limited impact of our life in community and of our curriculum redound to the glory of God and the health of his people, as individuals and as groups. We need the tenacity of bulldogs and the agility of butterflies if we are to be prompted by the Holy Spirit to play our small part well.

The collective mind of Virginia Seminary—whether bulldog-like or butterfly-like—has been shaped in part by its location. We have served a church of initially British ethnicity, subsequently engaging with the African-American population, and simultaneously encountering the cultures of Liberia, China, Japan, and Latin America. For our first century and a half we engaged non-Western cultures on their home territories. More recently we have engaged them as constituent parts of American society. Our engagement was not enough to avoid being noted by the Association of Theological Schools and by some of our African-American graduates for remaining too white. Thus spurred for the past six years to change our self-presentation and our ways, we have also been influenced by wider intellectual and political movements labeled "pluralism" or "multiculturalism."

Encountering Religions, Encountering Cultures

In the effort to evaluate and change one tiny subculture, is it possible that the cumulative experience of the Protestant era of Christian missions, of which Virginia Seminary is both heir and agent, might offer a source of guidance? After all, before the period of accelerated immigration to the United States that followed the 1950s, we had already been experiencing the encounter of cultures through our sustained missionary engagement overseas. To America's discussion about the meshing of subcultures today, I wish to offer the approach I have taken to Christians encountering live practitioners of non-biblical religions today. Religion may be only one component of a culture, confined to a limited domain. Religion may alternately be the source from which all behavior, ideas, and products in a culture derive. Either way, if religion, in its human aspect, belongs within culture, then the way I have been approaching other religions for the past twenty years could also be a way to approach the whole complex of other cultures and subcultures.

As a new teacher I fed Christian theological students Buddhism, Hinduism, and Islam in one large dose. After a decade of experience, it seemed more responsible to limit study to the two contrasting traditions of Hinduism and Islam. In the beginning I believed in the plunge: dive headfirst into the strangest culture. Begin in India with Hinduism, with its three hundred thirty million gods and its claim that Ultimate Reality and my inward internal self are not two things but one and the same. *Tat tvam asi.* That thou art. One and the same. Non-dual reality. Then turn and meet the Mother Goddess. She is the source of all energy, the destroyer of all evil, and the one whose grace saves me despite an immutable moral order where the karmic consequences of all human actions register on a reliably hierarchical universe. Welcome to India, home of Gandhi and of tolerance. Welcome to India, where those born outside the ritually pure castes are not fully human. Confused? Good. I believed that a strong dose of a coherent world view which has endured three millennia and cannot easily be squared with our biblical world view was a good place to start.

After a few more years I came to believe that putting Hinduism first was too disorienting and did not always encourage students to persevere into serious engagement. I reversed the order and began instead with Islam, which appears to share so much with a biblical view of reality. God is one. God has sent guidance and warning to human beings through many chosen messengers. Obedience, not birth, determines our ultimate destiny. So much seems familiar in the world of Islam that the more demanding part of the study is to dig until we discover Islam's optimistic view of human nature as able and ready to receive divine guidance. Gradually one uncovers doctrines like the eternal, uncreated Qur'an; the necessity of correct ritual cleansing from soles to nostrils before one's prayer can be heard; and the Sufi view of Jesus as an exemplary poor person with secret access to God.

Whether starting with the more familiar or the more alien, I asked students to proceed in three steps. The first step is immersion, trying to go deep rather than to attempt an overview or a summary. Plunge, but in a tiny tank. Pick one element from the code, or the cult, or the creed. It may be a purity rule. It may be a technique of meditation. It may be a doctrine about the scriptures of this tradition, or one key verse. Stick with your chosen element. Read how outside observers describe it. Listen to insiders. Taste it for yourself, if prudence permits. The first goal is to discover what the universe looks like when one brings into the foreground this particular element of one compelling, enduring, human tradition.

Crossing over is work. It is undertaken at some cost, perhaps with some fear of committing a disloyal act or falling under a power that might not let you go. I have had such feelings, spending the night alone in a Buddhist monastery on Lantau Island near Hong Kong, or being harangued outside a Banda Street mosque in Nairobi by a Muslim evangelist who had all the answers. I sympathize when students struggle. After a time of immersion, I encourage them to come back. I ask them to return, mentally and emotionally, into the biblical world, and the world of the Church, and there to reflect. What analogy can you discover between the element you have engaged in that other tradition and some element in our Christian tradition? Analogy is key. Each religious tradition has a distinct topography—its distinctive center, its own starting points, and its areas of heightened sensibility. Obvious analogies may mislead. Wilfred Cantwell Smith, the liberal Canadian scholar of Islam, alerted me to this when he pointed out that in Islam the closest parallel to Jesus is not Muhammad, though both may be understood as prophets. The closer analogue of Muhammad in Christian tradition, Smith said, is Mary—the willing, virgin receptor and transmitter of the divine Word into human form. Our effort to locate an apt Christian analogue for the element we have begun to appreciate in the other tradition demands empathy, some fresh laying-hold of our own tradition, and a bit of imagination.

The last move I ask of students is the most ticklish. We would omit this third step if I were teaching in a secular institution, because there the goals of study would not go beyond accurate understanding of our neighbors and promoting peace with them. Because my students are becoming pastors and teachers for the Christian community, they must take one more step. They must take a stand and reveal what is their own ultimate hope and confidence. Is the element you have come to understand in that other tradition compatible with the Christian tradition as you understand it? Here is the pastoral payoff from encountering world religions. Should I accept a drink of water previously used to render homage to the lineage of incarnations of Vishnu, when it is flavored with ash that signifies the burning away of illusory attachment to the human body as a thing of value? I personally decline the proffered water, but if a student can justify accepting the water, I accept that response. Was Muhammad God's inspired, final prophet and is the Qur'an God's final word for us? My own response is to affirm the early Meccan *surahs* and doubt the later Medinan *surahs*, but the student must choose his own standing place—and then live out the consequences of that stand.

Dual religious citizenship and hybrid cultural identity are hard to reconcile with an integrated human personality and the singularity of the God who revealed his name to Moses at the burning bush. The result of engaging across religious traditions is often a push and a push back, a "Yes" and a "No." We are likely to affirm some elements of the other tradition but still to reject some of its claims and practices, even when we have come to some understanding of why those claims and practices are necessary to the world view and way of life which that other religious tradition validates.

At least the goals for making the effort were clear. We sought to engage responsibly and sympathetically with the faith of neighbors who are not Christian. We aimed to clarify our views on the place of other religions in the providence, self-disclosure, and saving work of God. We tried to acquire information and skill to bring to bear in future interreligious encounters for which we may bear some responsibility.

Are these not akin to the goals of those who hope for the wheels of America's subcultures to engage?

Conclusion

I offer this Christian approach to world religions as also a way to approach the meshing of subcultures in American social institutions, including my own seminary. This approach goes one step beyond the method of the participant-observer. This approach invites individuals to reverse the order and add one step, becoming observer-participant-witnesses.

The observer-participant-witness defers judgment until he has tasted. He approaches another subgroup's culture appreciatively, expecting to discover and affirm how, yes, this too is a compelling and plausible way of being human in the world. He savors the other's tea, borrows his slippers, and wears them around awhile. At some point there arises the question of the observer-participant's home. The common room is good and necessary, but where do you live? The borrowed must be returned, or appropriated. The reporter's helicopter must land. I must name the place—the center of meaning, the point of density—where I live and move and have my being. I am finite, not omnilocal.

This final step of saying "Yes" to one element and "No" to another, of locating my standing ground and finding words for the hope I live by—this final step of testimony entails judgment, but judgment on all sides. As I search my own culture for analogues to the element in the other culture that has caught my eye, I may well stumble on a log in my own eye which I had never noticed. My fellows in the common room are likely to point out any log I miss. Being a witness includes self-examination and perhaps self-critique and repentance.

This method of engagement was tailored to Christians in America meeting Americans whose subculture is shaped, or once was shaped, or at least retains residual ideas, behaviors, and sacred objects received from a specific non-Christian religious tradition. Where religion permeates many domains of the subculture, it makes sense to seek to engage, appreciate, and assess that subculture via elements of its characteristic religious tradition. This method might serve Hindu and Muslim parents starting to explore with Christian parents, for example, their views on socializing between the sexes. Each group might begin by gathering accurate behavioral data, then working to empathize with practices that are offensive or opaque to them, and at some point rendering the inescapable declaration of where they as parents stand.

What if religion is only a minor domain among many domains comprising the subculture? Appalachian subculture may be more permeated than the general American culture with Christian ideas, but it is not obvious how a focus on Appalachian versions of the Christian tradition will help outsiders reckon well with, for example, Appalachian humor or Appalachian attitudes towards outsiders. Passion processions and Masses for the dead may strike outsiders as key elements in Hispanic-American culture, but how important are they really as centers of meaning? Religion may offer a more revealing entry point for understanding Salvadoran-American culture, say, than Puerto Rican or Cuban-American culture. The ethnographer, the community organizer, and the social institution who seek to welcome may have to try a variety of approaches before they begin to understand their neighbors.

For now the common room is still open. Who among us still dares act as the tea lady, presuming to care for the common room, making good its welcome by performing the received rites which make good on the promise of welcome? In the bustle of self-service, contests for seats, and negotiation between the ways others recognize us and the way we see and name ourselves, there might seem no role left for a keeper of the common. Clearly obsolete is the butler—announcing newcomers, assessing who belongs where, and keeping order in the house. That office has lost its authority.

The tea lady is different. She does not know in advance who will sit where, who will converse with whom, or who must give way to whom. She sees that the tea things are on hand and the room sufficiently tidy to encourage groups to stop in. Her efforts increase the chance that subgroups who make up the big group will in fact engage one another, will reflect each on its own identity, and will come to whatever stands are necessary regarding affirmation and conversion—whether of themselves or of others. So long as the tea lady is retained, others will have a place to discover which elements they can affirm in their neighbor's subculture and which they must resist.

So long as there is a tea lady, spoons can stir and gears can mesh.

Notes

1   Charles Taylor's *Multiculturalism and "The Politics of Recognition"* (Princeton, NJ: Princeton University Press, 1992) explores some of the unarticulated assumptions and unexplained concepts encountered in the current exaltation of ethnic diversity. A provocative sample of the far-ranging ideas of another Canadian, Wilfred Cantwell Smith, is the essay "Is the Qur'an the Word of God?" in his *Questions of Religious Truth* (Scribner's, 1967).

     The cultural border-crosser who has most influenced me is Kenneth Cragg, whose Sprigg Lectures delivered in 1985 at Virginia Seminary on this subject were published as *Christ in Cross-Reference* (SPCK, 1986), and who tells his own story in *Faith and Life Negotiate* (Canterbury Press, Norwich, 1994). James Wood's review of Richard Peaver and Larissa Volokhonsky's translation of *War and Peace* appeared in the November 26, 2007, issue of the *New Yorker Magazine.* On the notions of domains and themes in a culture, see James P. Spradley's handbook for ethnographic research, *Participant Observation* (Holt Rinehart, 1980).

2   Paul G. Hieber, *Cultural Anthropology* (Grand Rapids, MI: Baker Book House, 1983), 25.

3   Franklin Giddings, *Principles of Sociology* (New York: The Macmillan Company, 1921), 17.

4   Taylor, *Multiculturalism and "The Politics of Recognition,"* 36, 26.

International Students at Virginia Seminary: A Long History with a Rich and Transformative Practice

James Barney Hawkins IV

In May 1994 the Board of Trustees of Virginia Theological Seminary elected the Very Rev. Martha J. Horne dean and president. At the time the Rt. Rev. Peter James Lee, the Chair of the Board of Trustees, noted that "a new chapter of fidelity, and change required by that fidelity, has begun."[1] In the 1995 foreword to Professor John E. Booty's *Mission and Ministry: A History of Virginia Theological Seminary*, Bishop Lee foretold the Seminary's coming agenda: "The seminary will look to new ways to equip God's people for mission and ministry, and will wrestle with questions unimagined by the founders. The seminary will take risks because risk taking . . . is part of what it means to be faithful."[2]

It is true that the Seminary in the Horne years sought "new ways to equip God's people" in a church and culture which were changing dramatically. Without a doubt, the Seminary's community of trustees, faculty, staff, alumni/ae, friends, and the wider church wrestled "with questions unimagined by the founders," such as the place of gays and lesbians in the life of the Episcopal Church. At the same time the Seminary remained steady in its long-standing commitment to educate and equip international students for service in the Anglican Communion and beyond.

This paper will provide a summative history of the Seminary's first missionaries and the international students who came after them. There will be reflections on the original impetus for the presence of international students on the Holy Hill and the way in which the Seminary has evolved in its mission and ministry with and for international students. It is an inspiring story with a history almost as long as the Seminary's. The practice of welcoming and educating international students makes for a rich narrative, and the Seminary's engagement with international students has shaped the institution in transformative ways.

The class of 1995 was the first to graduate in the Horne years. They and others gave the Miriam Window in Immanuel Chapel in thanksgiving for the teaching, ministry, and faithful witness of three Old Testament professors. The Miriam Window depicts Miriam, with tambourine, in the company of four other women with their own instruments—playing, singing, and dancing. The hem of Miriam's garment has in Hebrew the words from Exodus 15:21: "Sing to the Lord for he hath triumphed gloriously." The hills and rivers of the Holy Land are the background for this window, which celebrates "Israel's freedom from bondage in Egypt as the Israelites crossed the Red Sea to safety."[3]

The Miriam Window and its dedication capture much of the historical significance of the Horne years: the increasing role of women in the life of the Episcopal Church; the ever-present emphasis on the study of the Bible in the core Seminary curriculum; the inseparable connection between the life of the mind and the journey of faith; and the deep connection in the Seminary's life to the biblical narrative and the mission of the church. Indeed, it is this last witness in the Miriam Window which was a founding principle in the Seminary's early decision to welcome international students to campus and to serve well beyond the borders of the Episcopal Church in the United States.

The connection between the biblical narrative and the mission of the church is also articulated in the Altar Window of Immanuel Chapel. The window with a city in the background interprets the brief return visit of Jesus with the eleven disciples after his Ascension (Mark 16:14–15). He tells them to "Go into all the world and proclaim the good news to the whole creation" (NRSV). If the text of the window itself were not enough, the Seminary has painted a border for the window on the white wall: "Go ye into all the world, and preach the gospel to every creature" (KJV). The window with its biblical text as a frame has become iconic for the Seminary, suggestive of its deepest purpose and mission as an institution. Both the Miriam Window and the mission-dominated Altar Window celebrate the Seminary's long history and mission practice in the Episcopal Church and the Anglican Communion.

In his 1923 history of the Seminary, W.A.R. Goodwin wrote: "The chief glory of the Theological Seminary in Virginia has been her loyalty and devotion to the mission of the Church."[4] In the early years graduates went out to Greece, China, and Liberia. In time there were Seminary graduates in Japan and Brazil. But also there was a strong desire, even in the early years, to serve the Church by bringing international students to study on the Holy Hill. There is, though Seminary graduates rarely go as missionaries to a foreign country upon graduation, a robust, if not growing, residential program of formation and study for international students that became more diverse in the late 1960s and early 1970s. Increasingly, Virginia Seminary understands mission as equipping international students to lead and to serve in their homelands rather than sending its graduates as missionaries of the Church.

The first missionaries to go out from the Seminary paved the way for the international students who continue to come to the campus for study. The Seminary's first foreign missionary was the Rev. John H. Hill, class of 1830, who with his wife, Frances Maria, went to Greece after his graduation. Hill was appointed by the Domestic and Foreign Missionary Society of the Protestant Episcopal Church, and he remained in Greece for almost fifty-two years. He and his wife were determined from the start not to offend the Greek Orthodox Church. Much of their focus was on education, and they founded a school in 1831 which had a thousand students within a decade. The Hill missionary team of husband and wife "never attempted to undermine the religious convictions of their pupils, but they even took conscientious care to strengthen the same."[5] From the beginning, the missionary impulse embedded in the Seminary's commitment to "go ye into all the world and preach the gospel" was shaped by tolerance for those with differing "religious convictions." Conversion to the Christian faith is boldly embedded in the Seminary's understanding of the mission of the Church. But for John and Frances Maria Hill, conversation with the Orthodox was always front and center, education was the focus, and respectful tolerance was the hallmark of their missionary service. These first missionaries from the Seminary, lay and ordained, laid a very good foundation for those who would come after them as students on the Holy Hill. The Hills embodied what has been best in an Anglican rendering of the mission of the Church: education, conversation, tolerance, and respect for difference.

In 1833, a decade after the seminary was founded, the Rev. Francis R. Hanson, newly graduated, set out for China, but illness forced him to return to the States a year later. Another graduate, the Rev. William J. Boone (class of 1835) actually began the mission of the Episcopal Church in China, which became the crown jewel of missionary efforts in the nineteenth century. In 1844 Boone was elected the Bishop of Amoy and Other Parts of China and is well remembered because of his missionary zeal coupled with a "concentration" on indigenous ordained ministry.[6] A number of Chinese students would later come to the Seminary for their theological education and formation as church leaders because of Boone's faithful witness.

The American Civil War wreaked havoc on the lives of all associated with the Seminary, and "it also hindered the flow of money from the United States to the Chinese mission. Many church-sponsored schools closed in China during this period, and all but two American missionaries returned . . . to the United States."[7] The latter decades of the nineteenth century saw very few of the Seminary's graduates embarking for China as missionaries. In Goodwin's history, he notes that since 1891 there had been a steady supply of clergy to China from the Seminary—normally at least one in each graduating class, with Virginia Seminary supplying over 42 percent of the clergy sent to China.[8] This steady stream of missionaries continued until the Chinese revolution in 1949, which resulted in the banning of any further religious personnel and the expelling of all expatriate missionaries.

In 1909 the Seminary opened its doors to the first international student from China. From 1924 to 1949 the Seminary had six students from China. Virginia Seminary, along with many other Christian institutions, sent numbers of priests and missionaries to China in the nineteenth century, and, as the mission in China matured, local Chinese students were selected to study at places like the Seminary. Language barriers and cultural differences complicated this important missionary engagement—which may account for the small number of Chinese students who actually enrolled at the Virginia Seminary.

Three graduates of the Seminary, Lancelot B. Minor, John Payne, and Thomas Savage, traveled to West Africa in 1836 for mission work on the southern shore of Liberia. After fifteen years as a missionary, the Rev. John Payne was elected Bishop of Cape Palmas and Parts Adjacent and returned to Virginia for his episcopal consecration. On the return trip, his fellow travelers, "Mr. G.T. Bedell and an unnamed student," were the Seminary's first non-European international students. Dr. James May, Seminary professor (1842–1861), hosted these first international students. Bedell stayed only a year and returned to Liberia where he served as a priest until his death in 1897. The Seminary's hospitality to international students began because of Seminary graduates whose missionary efforts included the cultivation of potential theological students who could study at Virginia Seminary.[9]

Bedell and the unnamed students were African students and were not officially enrolled at the Seminary. Probably because of segregation, these students were privately tutored in the Mays' home. So, the first international students were not full-fledged students. Yet, with Bedell's time on campus, 1852–1853, the Seminary commenced its long tradition of welcoming students from foreign lands to "study, reflect and pray at Virginia Theological Seminary."[10] Bedell was the first of many students from Liberia who found the Seminary a place of formation, training, and education.

It would not be until the 1950s that students from Liberia were allowed to attend the Seminary officially because of segregation laws in Virginia and the American South. The first fully enrolled student from Liberia in this modern era was Samuel Dennis, who came to live at the Seminary in 1954, just over a hundred years after Mr. G. T. Bedell lived on campus as an unofficial student. Dennis, an international student from Africa, was enrolled just three years after the Seminary admitted in 1951 its first African-American student, John T. Walker, who became the Bishop of Washington.[11]

In the spirit of the Miriam Window, Theodora Brooks, who graduated from the Seminary in 1992, became the first woman ordained in the Episcopal Church in Liberia. The civil war in Liberia from 1999 to 2003 disrupted the Seminary's communications and relations with the Church in Liberia. The Rev. Edward Gbe's enrollment in 2007, Horne's last year, symbolized the return of Liberian students to the Seminary, a tradition that has included at least nineteen students.

Japan was closed to foreigners until Commodore Perry of the United States sailed into Tokyo Bay in 1853 and demanded a trading agreement. Shortly thereafter, three Episcopal missionaries from China were transferred to Japan, two of whom were Virginia Seminary graduates, the class of 1855. The Rev. John Liggins and the Rev. Channing Moore Williams are remembered in Neill's history: "The Christianity in Japan today goes back to these two men, the first Protestant missionaries ever to land in Japan, the first founders of all modern Japanese Christianity of any sort."[12] Both Liggins and Williams "concentrated on the 'civilizing' activities of schools and hospitals, rather than any direct evangelistic outreach."[13] Once again, it seems that the great commission or command of Jesus is about conversation as much as it is about conversion for Anglican/ Episcopal missionaries. The mission of the Church is about conversion—but it is also about education, conversation, toleration, and respect for difference.

Throughout the nineteenth century, the Episcopal Church in the United States controlled the two largest dioceses in the *Nippon Sei Ko Kai*, literally the Japanese Holy Catholic Church, the Diocese of Tokyo and the Diocese of Kyoto. Most Japanese students who have attended the Seminary have been from one of these dioceses, often associated with a graduate of Virginia Seminary who became a missionary. Our first Japanese student, Isaac Yokoyama, arrived in 1875.[14] For twelve years, from 1938 to 1950, because of World War II, there were no Japanese students at the Seminary. Over the years the Seminary has trained at least thirty Japanese students, but the numbers from Japan began to wane in the mid-1960s. One Japanese student, the Rev. Peter Hamaya, graduated the year before Dean Horne was elected. No Japanese students studied at the Seminary during the Horne years, although the Rev. Kevin Seaver, an American who spoke fluent Japanese, graduated in 2003. The Rev. Seaver had lived in Japan prior to attending

Seminary and married a Japanese woman. Upon graduation, he returned to Japan.

In 1859 the American Church Missionary Society was formed to promote a more evangelical polity in the Episcopal Church. Some fifteen years later, a group of Virginia Seminary students joined the Inter-Seminary Mission Alliance, which sought to create a "missionary spirit among theological students" with a focus on Brazil, Cuba, and Mexico. It was thought that the language barrier in Central and South America was minimal, compared to China and Japan, "where the languages are the most difficult in the world." [15]

Once again and assisted by the American Church Missionary Society, two Virginia Seminary graduates, the Revs. Lucien Kinsolving and James Morris, set out for Brazil in 1889.[16] Like graduates who had gone to China, Greece, Japan, and Liberia, the missionaries to Brazil focused on building up a self-supporting native church, converting and training a native ministry and providing for Christian schools. It was not until 1932 that the first international student from Brazil arrived in Alexandria to study at the Seminary. Seven others followed, and the last Brazilian to study at the Seminary graduated in 1968. Episcopal missionary work began in Cuba in 1871. Virginia Seminary has welcomed eight Cubans as Seminary students, but none since 1959.[17]

Students from Mexico who came to the Seminary to study did not derive from a missionary effort fostered by Virginia Seminary graduates. Goodwin's history records that a graduate in the 1890s concluded that "the condition of Mexico, with its degrading superstitions and low standard of morals" was unsuitable for missionary support.[18] The first student arrived from Mexico to study at the Seminary in 1943. But like Brazil and Cuba, Mexico has provided only six students, and none since 1986.

In the late 1960s and early 1970s, international students began coming to the Seminary from countries that did not have connections with Virginia Seminary through its historical missionary efforts. This shift at the Seminary coincides with a decline in missionary appointments by the Episcopal Church in the United States and increased communication within the Anglican Communion, as a result of the first meeting of the Anglican Consultative Council in 1971. The initial meeting of the Council provided a time "to talk together, work together, worship together and live together in a mature family of churches." It was a time of growth in the Anglican Communion but also a time of a diminished Church of England influence worldwide. Kenya, Tanzania, and Burma became independent of the Anglican Church in England in 1970. They sought new partners for mission and ministry with a new vision of the missionary task. Other Anglican dioceses emerged, such as Sudan in 1976. So, Virginia Seminary opened its doors to students from Ethiopia (1967), Gambia (1968), Nigeria and Cameroon (1969), the Philippines (1970), Korea (1973), Tanzania (1976), Malawi and the Sudan (1978), Namibia, South Africa and Botswana (1982), Kenya and Israel (1986), Myanmar (1987), Ghana (1992), Bolivia (1994), Zambia and Ecuador (1995), and Rwanda (1997).[19]

By the mid-1970s, Africa became the primary partner continent for the international-students program at Virginia Seminary. The Anglican Church in Tanzania has sent more students to the Seminary than any other country in Africa. Twenty-one students from Tanzania have studied at the Seminary and eight during the Horne deanship. The leadership of the Anglican Church in Tanzania has been shaped strongly by the teaching ministry of Virginia Seminary. The deep association with Tanzania was the impetus for the Very Rev. Martha J. Horne's final overseas trip as dean—to give the commencement address at Msalato Bible College in Dodoma, Tanzania, in 2007. Tanzanian graduates of the Seminary traveled miles to connect with Dean Horne and the Seminary she represented. The current dean, the Very Rev. Ian S. Markham, traveled to the same Anglican institution to give the commencement address in June 2009.

There is also a long connection between the Seminary and the Anglican Church in Sudan. This association comes out of that fertile time of transition in the late 1960s and early 1970s and the Mutual Responsibility and Interdependence Programs created by the Anglican Communion. The Seminary can trace its own involvement with Sudan to the Diocese of Southwestern Virginia and the leadership of the Rt. Rev. Heath Light, who encouraged Sudanese applications to Virginia Seminary. The first student from Sudan, the Rev. Eluzai Munda, arrived in 1978.[20] During the Horne years and largely because of Professors Ellen Davis and Richard Jones, the Seminary has forged a strong link with the Theological College in Renk where Virginia Seminary students teach biblical languages in an ongoing partnership. Seminary students visiting and teaching in a sister seminary of the Anglican Communion may be another model for connecting with international students and sharing in the mission and ministry of the Church.

Since 1987, when the Rt. Rev. John Wilme was a student at the Seminary, there has been a lively partnership between Virginia Seminary and the Anglican Church in Myanmar/ Burma. Six Burmese students have studied at the Seminary, including one who received a Doctor of Ministry degree and now is the Principal of Holy Cross Theological School, which is a continuing partner with the Seminary in its missionary work in Myanmar/Burma. Indeed, Virginia Seminary is focusing more and more on strategic academic partners as it equips international students to serve on the faculties of theological schools. There is a noticeable shift from the education of international students as pastors to the education of church scholars and leaders for the larger Church. A similar shift in purpose occurred during the Horne years as the Seminary sought to form leaders, not pastors, for the Church in general.

As American missionaries first embarked for distant lands, the impetus was to win the world for Christ—and, to be honest, to export American values and ideals. It does appear that missionaries trained at Virginia Seminary were sensitive to the cultural differences and educational needs of the people to whom they preached the Good News of Jesus Christ. The missionaries' task was both conversion and conversation.

It has been noted, with sadness at times, that international students are often exposed to the ways of Virginia Seminary more than Virginia Seminary is exposed to the diverse ways of the students who bring many forms of cultural diversity to the campus and its community life. To say it another way: The international student learns more about American culture than Virginia Seminary and its students learn about the different culture of the international student. The Seminary focuses on training leaders for the Anglican Communion—but too often that has been a one-way street. There has always been an emphasis on coexistence with the other, but the Seminary has not always done a good job of helping international students understand American culture.[21] By the same token, the Seminary community has not always taken the time to understand the culture out of which the international student has come.

A survey of international graduates in 2008 discovered that some international students have found only a North American or White-European perspective in the classroom. One respondent to the survey attributed the narrow cultural vantage point to the limited international exposure of faculty and staff.[22] In the last ten years and during the Horne tenure, the Seminary made considerable strides in cross-cultural education and formation for all students. Cultural differences are named, examined, and discussed. Differing theological perspectives are recognized, and diverse ways of approaching the biblical narrative are respected and explored.

While the 2008 survey of international graduates identified weaknesses in the Seminary's long-standing commitment to the education and formation of international students, there was much that was positive in the feedback from international graduates. Graduates who have returned to their home country express gratitude that at Virginia Seminary they learned the importance of learning as a "life-long, continual process."[23]

Others praised the level of educational instruction and the desire for more education which they attribute to their time at Virginia Seminary. A number of respondents to the survey have come to see their education at the Seminary as leadership training that focused on knowledge and resources. There has been a steady shift from pastoral training to leadership training for all students at the Seminary. Of note was the comment by one international graduate that Virginia Seminary helped him to "preach to Muslims and relate to those of different faiths."[24]

So, Virginia Seminary remains strongly committed to the formation and education of international students. The Seminary's history with this effort has revealed that international students bring a cultural perspective, indeed a life story, which must be understood, appreciated, and heard. When a priest from Tanzania sings the Lord's song, as in the Miriam Window, it will be different from the song of a student from Kansas or Alabama or Myanmar/Burma. Cross-cultural listening and learning are critical as the Seminary shapes church leaders for leadership in diverse cultures and in churches which have very different perspectives on the biblical narrative and the Christian tradition. The earliest missionaries who went out from Virginia Seminary were committed to conversation, education, tolerance, and the deep connection between the life of the mind and the journey of faith. A similar constellation of concerns has come to shape the Seminary's community life and its deliberate incorporation of international students, mindful of the faith we share and the differences we must acknowledge.

A theological reflection on Virginia Seminary's international efforts suggests that the desire to connect the biblical narrative to the mission of the Church is motivated by Jesus' post-Ascension command to his disciples to "go ye into all the world and preach the gospel." Over time, that noble incentive to make disciples in every age and on every continent has transformed the community which is Virginia Seminary. It is a worldwide community of church leaders. Truly the world has become the Seminary's parish. Because of the Seminary's

Staying One, Remaining Open

international vision, life on the Holy Hill is different in countless ways, from the cuisine served in the refectory to the resources used in the classroom to the prayers which are uttered in Immanuel Chapel. In many ways the Seminary has become a microcosm of the Anglican Communion, diverse, divided, and vibrant. For the most part, international students who study at Virginia Seminary are poorer, less educated, and more conservative than most of the North American students. Diversity brings a range of theological opinions and perspectives. The presence of international students at the Seminary has forced the community to live with a divided mind, fundamental difference, and unavoidable tension.

The Miriam Window was dedicated as the deanship of the Very Rev. Martha J. Horne began. A few years later, in 1999, as a century of mission and ministry came to a close at Virginia Seminary, the Gibson Windows were dedicated. Dean Horne has said that the windows "pay tribute to all who have responded to the missionary charge of Jesus: 'Go ye into all the world and preach the gospel'" and "invite us to remember those who have gone forth from this Seminary to proclaim the gospel to people far and near."[25] While the international vision of the Seminary encompasses many lands and people, the Gibson Windows highlight the missionary outreach of the Seminary in Africa, North America, Central America, and Asia. The first window recalls the Seminary's deep roots in Africa and the inseparable connection between the biblical narrative and the mission of the Church. The second Gibson Window celebrates with a small blue airplane the ever-changing, evolving mission and ministry of the Church, particularly in North America. The third window with its image of Central America captures the geographical and cultural diversity of the Seminary's international vision for the whole Church. The final window finds missionaries beside the waters of baptism and a cross in the sky above an Asian temple, reminding the Seminary who gathers for worship in Immanuel Chapel that cultural context always matters as the gospel is preached.

The Gibson Windows enshrine in Immanuel Chapel the Seminary's timeless commitment to preach the gospel "to people far and near." As Bishop Lee said at the beginning of the Horne years, the seminary will always look "to new ways to equip God's people for mission and ministry" and it "will take risks because risk taking . . . is part of what it means to be faithful."[26] Being faithful for Virginia Seminary has always included mission and ministry that are connected to an international community. The Seminary has been steadily transformed by its engagement with the Anglican Communion and the larger Church. It is an engagement which is biblically mandated, theologically informed, and tradition-constituted. The Horne years confirmed that Virginia Seminary is a seminary at the heart of the Episcopal Church. International students at Virginia Seminary confirm that it has been and always will be a seminary for the Anglican Communion, the larger Church, and the whole world. Virginia Seminary has been shaped, changed, and transformed by the missionaries who have gone forth from its campus and by the international students who have steadily arrived at its campus for theological education and formation for service in Christ's larger Church. Disciples in every age have obeyed the command of Jesus, as Virginia Seminary obeys in its time: "Go ye into all the world and preach the gospel."

Notes

1 John E. Booty, *Mission and Ministry: A History of Virginia Theological Seminary* (Harrisburg, PA: Morehouse Publishing, 1995), x.

2 Booty.

3 Alix Dorr, ed., *O Gracious Light: Stained Glass Windows in Immanuel Chapel—Virginia Theological Seminary* (Alexandria, VA: Charter Printing Service, 2000), 28.

4 W.A.R. Goodwin, ed., *History of the Theological Seminary in Virginia and Its Historical Background* (New York: Gorham, 1923), vol. 1, 171.

5   Troy D. Mendez, "A History of Mission: International Students and Virginia Theological Seminary," paper prepared for an independent study with the Rev. J. Barney Hawkins IV, 2008, 3.

6   Booty, 64.

7   Mendez, "A History of Mission," 8.

8   Mendez, 9.

9   Booty, 64.

10 Mendez, "A History of Mission," 6.

11 Mendez, 6.

12 Stephen Neill, *A History of Christian Missions* (New York: Penguin Books, 1964), 324–25.

13 Mendez, "A History of Mission," 10.

14 Mendez, 12.

15 Mendez, 14–17.

16 Ian Theodore Douglas, *Fling Out the Banner: The National Church Ideal and the Foreign Mission of the Episcopal Church* (Ann Arbor, MI: UMI Dissertation Services, 1996), 80.

17 Mendez, "A History of Mission," 17.

18 Mendez, 18.

19 Mendez, 24.

20 Mendez, 28.

21 Troy Mendez, "Survey of International Students at Virginia Theological Seminary," undertaken as part of an independent study with the Rev. J. Barney Hawkins IV, 2008, 2.

22 Mendez, "Survey," 13.

23 Mendez, "Survey," 7.

24 Mendez, "Survey," 10.

25 Dorr, ed., 3.

26 Booty, x.

The Theologian Is
the One Who Prays

Timothy F. Sedgwick

Evagrius Ponticus in the fourth century said, "The theologian is the one who prays truly, and the one who prays truly is a theologian."[1] The relationship of prayer and belief is similarly raised by Prosper of Aquitaine in the fifth century in the oft-quoted maxim in liturgical theology: *lex orandi, lex credendi,* the law or order of prayer is the law or order of belief.[2] This earliest tradition in Christian theology simply could not separate belief and prayer. We know something or someone—like we know those we love—only in relationship. As an analogy, we may be able to name members of our family and know that they have deeply shaped our lives; however, we know them only as we sit around a table together and share our cares and concerns, loves and hopes. So our relationship with God is known in prayer and worship. Theology as the study of God depends upon a spiritual life. Contemporary theological education—and specifically the education of those who would lead congregations centered in the worship of God—requires that prayer and worship be at its center.

This fundamental claim that theology and prayer cannot be separated stands in sharp contrast to the contemporary study of theology, at least in its university setting. There, under the claims of objectivity—as in scientific and historical disciplines—the study of God is the study of claims and counterclaims within the tradition. Whether the question is the meaning of the word "God" or what it means to claim that God is incarnate in Christ, university theology seeks to understand why claims have been made and what they could mean now. Theology is historical, comparative, and critical. Prayer can have no place as source or referent to claims about God.

Perhaps, however, theology as a divine science is more like poetry than the natural or social sciences. The knowledge of God is personal knowledge.[3] We know God as we know persons, not as physiological organisms, but as persons whom we come to know by sharing and participating in the meanings and purposes of their lives. As H. Richard Niebuhr commented, "We have prejudices in favor of impersonal categories, as though the impersonal were more likely to characterize existence than the personal, as though thinghood were more original than self-hood . . . our fundamental attitude, however, is personal."[4]

In understanding the knowledge of God in such a frame of reference, the first question is spiritual: what are the spiritual disciplines by which we theologize, by which we come to the knowledge of God? In such knowledge, of course, there is a play between *lex orandi, lex credendi.* How does or should theology as the statement and exploration of what we believe inform, fund, and give rise to prayer? How does or should prayer (along with other spiritual exercises) inform, fund, and give rise to thought and reflection on the nature of God and on how God is present in our world and our lives? The answers to these questions stand at the heart of theological education, at least for any theological education that seeks to educate and form teachers of the faith who are able to invite people into the knowledge of God rather than philosophers of religion who traffic in ideas about God.

The education of religious scholars—theologians in the broadest sense of the term, beginning with biblical scholars—has to a great extent adopted a historical, critical, comparative approach that seeks to understand the origin of beliefs in terms of history and interest. Given historical description, beliefs and practices are understood as shaped by the interests and power of certain actors, for example, as patriarchal, misogynist, Eurocentric, and colonial. Underlying such critiques is a normative (Enlightenment) view that holds to a view of human equality and human rights. Such an approach is especially appealing where teaching religion in colleges and universities is not supposed to be partisan but (supposedly) "objective." As doctoral programs at universities see their mission to provide scholars and teachers for such universities (rather than for seminaries as was the case through the mid-twentieth century), religious practices and spiritual exercises are separated from theological studies. What was once assumed—students who daily worshiped, prayed, and read scripture—is lost (at least from view) and assumed irrelevant to the study of religion. To the extent that a historical, critical, comparative approach to religion determines scholarship in the various fields of theological study, the education of religious leaders suffers. They are unable to invite others into relationship with God or else, more likely, do so with a fideism on the side of belief and a magical supernaturalism on the side of prayer.

The challenge for theological education in general and for seminary education of leaders for Christian communities in particular is to ensure an integration of theology and spiritual exercises in understanding and practice.[5]

Theology and the Conversation of Prayer

Drawing on Philo and other ancient philosophers who list practices which shape the self and the way in which we come to relate to and know the world about us, Pierre Hadot speaks of spiritual exercises of mind and body.[6] Much like the lover knows the beloved, these disciplines are the way we know God.

The central spiritual exercises of the mind are the practices of contemplation and meditation. Contemplation is an exercise in memory. For example, when looking upon a line of scripture (as in *lectio divina*), a painting, stained-glass window, or an icon (such as Rublev's icon of the Holy Trinity), we hold something in attention, we keep it in mind. This is variously a matter of enjoyment, a matter of association, a matter of seeing more deeply. The tradition speaks of this as *kataphatic* prayer, praying with images. This process has been elucidated by Edmund Husserl's phenomenological investigation in which he describes the primary process of perception as a matter of appresentation. By this he means the immediate pairing in consciousness of what is seen with what is remembered. For example, in seeing a box, the front side is paired in consciousness with a backside so that we see a box instead of a trompe l'oeil, as with a William Harnett one-dimensional painting of a box. And so we may hold before us what we see in a moment or we may give free play in "a stream of consciousness," a range of associations, stopping at various points to give further attention and direction to our consciousness.[7]

Contemplation as a form of knowing is complemented by what are called *apophatic* forms of prayer, literally forms of prayer without images. As is emphasized in forms of Buddhist meditation, by withdrawing attention from the objects of consciousness, we become "mindless" and have a sense of consciousness itself. As Buddhism claims, this consciousness may be identified with consciousness of Being itself, a sense of pure presence. As in centering prayer, apophatic forms of prayer clear the mind and may give a sense of the presence and power of God beyond all words. At the least, they ground our thoughts and ideas about God and convince the self of the ultimate incomprehensibility of God and the limitations of thought.

A second set of disciplines of the mind are what ancients speak about as conversation and examination. Contemplation leads to conversation between text or the object of contemplation and the reader or worshiper. I may contemplate the starry heavens, but then I ask the question, "What does this say or mean for me? Who am I and what is my purpose in the midst of this vast universe?"

Both ancients and contemporaries understand that reading is fundamentally a form of conversation. The story of the Good Samaritan tells how religious practices push moral obligations to the side. Juxtaposition and surprise raise questions for the reader, especially as she identifies with the different characters in the story. In the parable of the Prodigal Son (and the profligate father), the reader may identify with both father and son. He not only may wonder about his wanderings away from home directed by his own desires, but he may question how he has welcomed his son or daughter.

Such conversations are themselves an examination of the self. In fact, following Soren Kierkegaard, Jacques Derrida has claimed that what is distinctive about the gospels is that they initiate a radical questioning of the self so that we seek a unity of thought and action, desire and duty. In hearing that "Your Father who sees in secret will reward you" (Matthew 6:4b, 6b, 16b), the reader examines all actions to identify and cast out evil intentions and to identify and deepen the singleness of desire as love.[8] Disciplines of examination are refined in forms of confession, beginning with Augustine's *Confessions*, where he seeks to tell the story of his life by identifying the particular events of his life in terms of desire. For example, in his *Confessions* Augustine describes his stealing of a pear and throwing it away in terms of what he desired. What was initially a carefree act becomes a capricious and gratuitous act, evidence of a wanton will.[9] Each act raises the question of what is really desired. In the very questioning, desire is to be unified and the self is formed as a unity of desire. Examination then transforms the self into a unified subject who seeks to find her rest in God as Creator and Redeemer, beginning and end.

While God pervades our life, the knowledge of God (literally, theology) only comes to us through these disciplines of the mind—whether exercised explicitly or implicitly. Contemplation and meditation and conversation and examination connect the faith that has been given us with our lived experience of being in the world. The deposit of faith given as scripture and tradition isn't personal knowledge of God until this connection is made. For example, our beliefs about God—as good and sovereign ruler over all instead of as being both good and evil—inform and effect what we see and how we examine our selves and the world about us. In turn, our experience and understanding of the world shape and deepen, as well as modify or even change, our beliefs about God—for example, what we mean by good and sovereign ruler.[10] Theology as the knowledge of God is this play between spiritual exercises and theological beliefs or, again, it is what liturgical theologians have expressed as a matter of *lex orandi, lex credendi*. And this means, as Evagrius said, "The theologian is the one who prays truly, and the one who prays truly is a theologian."[11]

The Body and the Knowledge of God

In his account of spiritual exercises of late antiquity, Hadot distinguishes between spiritual exercises of the mind and spiritual exercises of the body. In fact, practices of the mind are dependent on the practices of the body. We are conscious of and reflect upon that which we know through the body. Light and dark, sound and smell, taste and touch—we sense the world only through the body. Only through the body are we in touch with the world. In turn, only through the body do we act in the world, connecting to others and acting upon them and the world about us. Consciousness and freedom of action: these two features are central to what we mean when we speak of the human spirit. They are, however, never independent of the body. This is what we mean when we say that we are embodied. Body and spirit are inseparable. "We are embodied spirits, inspirited bodies."[12] Theological education as the knowledge of God requires exercise of the body as much as the exercises of the mind.

Exercises of the body may be negative or positive acts. Negative acts are negative in the sense that they restrain or negate something in order to direct or redirect the experience of the self and ultimately shape desire. These actions are traditionally spoken about as matters of asceticism, as acts of denial and purgation. Among ancients the three central acts of denial and purgation were fasting, sexual renunciation, and bodily mortification. In withdrawing what meets our basic bodily functions, we purge ourselves from inordinate desire so that our desire may be redirected to what is true, good, and enduring. More broadly, a contemporary asceticism is a matter of simplification of life by withdrawing from being "tuned-in" all the time to others and to the broader commodification of daily life, the creation of needs in order to sell products. Ascetic disciplines offer a defense against what Paul speaks about as the world, what the later Christian tradition speaks about as the fallen world. More than defense, however, ascetic disciplines create space so that the self can attend to other possibilities and feel again or anew its deeper desires.[13]

Positive bodily exercises are positive in the sense that they offer a positive experience of what fulfills and should direct human desire. These exercises are what ancients spoke about as duties. They are sacramental in character. For example, Christians have claimed that table fellowship, welcoming the stranger, feeding the hungry, caring for the sick, visiting those in prison, and forgiving those who have acted against us

(Matthew 25:34–40) are actions by which we know God. These are duties in the sense that they are what bind us to God. They are sacramental in that in signifying what we are meant to be, they draw us into the experience of the presence of God.[14]

Spiritual exercises of the body may be divided into the religious, and specifically those of worship, and those that are moral, directed towards another. For example, while the Eucharist has within it practices of contemplation, meditation, and examination—such as the reading of scripture, the prayers of the people, and joining in the Eucharistic Prayer—the Eucharist is also a set of bodily disciplines. These may begin with a fast before receiving communion and certainly include sharing together in communion. As directed towards God, practices of worship are distinct from practices focused in response to the needs of the other, such as feeding the hungry and caring for the sick. Here again, though, the bodily practice signifies and effects the presence of God in our lives.

Spiritual exercises of mind and spiritual exercises of body assume the primacy of lived experience, whether engaged in memory as exercises of the mind or as shaped by exercises of the body. We are "embodied spirits, inspired bodies."[15] This is the primary theology that Evagrius Ponticus and Prosper of Aquitaine speak about. The theologian is one who prays. Worship is primary theology. Theology is reflection upon such experience. Similarly, liturgical theologians have focused on the primacy of the act. While we can always refer to Augustine, Anglican Dom Gregory Dix reflects this understanding in his 1948 classic, *The Shape of the Liturgy*. In Anglicanism in general, this line of thought has been central to what is called *kenotic* theology, specifically as that tradition is begun in F.D. Maurice, developed explicitly in Charles Gore, and further developed in the thought of Archbishops William Temple, Michael Ramsey, and Rowan Williams. It is also significantly developed in the current work of theologians Sarah Coakley and Mark McIntosh.[16]

Kenotic theology arose in response to the problem of modernism and the historical character of scripture, especially the question of how to understand the atonement, how Christ's death on the cross is redemptive, and what then is the meaning of the resurrection and life everlasting. The answer is not to be found in some speculative claims about the eschaton and bodily resurrection. Instead, these theologians make the turn to the subject and understand that the salvific nature of the cross is given in Christ's self-offering (*kenosis*) as the revelation of a perfect or complete relationship with God. Christ's self-offering "unto death, even death on the cross" (Philippians 2:8, KJV) is the revelation of what it is to be reconciled and in union with God. This experience of offering or sacrifice is not the denial but the full realization of the self in relationship to others. In this way atonement is exemplary: Christ reveals God's redemptive intent and so draws us into the offering of ourselves to God.

From Maurice to Dix to many contemporary sacramental theologians, the atonement as *kenosis* is what is effected in the Eucharist. In the Eucharist the congregation offers itself to God in Christ and through Christ. In this offering the self is emptied, reconciled, and united with God. Here is an understanding that the knowledge of God is pre-reflective. It is the experience of God, which is at the heart of our lives, that is celebrated and effected in worship and most centrally in the Eucharist. Theological reflection is funded or grounded in this experience. It is assumed as the necessary condition of theological reflection.

The consequence of this line of reflection is again that theological reflection and spiritual formation are integral. But here there is even greater primacy on disciplines of the body. The knowledge of God depends upon spiritual exercises/disciplines and not simply on the disciplines of the mind. In fact, the disciplines of the mind as a matter of remembering evidence a certain priority of the body over the mind. If our bodily experience of God is not sustained, we lose sight of God from consciousness, and theology moves to the speculative and often scholastic. The implications for seminary education—for educating persons to be leaders in the community of faith—is radical, at least in relationship to university-based religious studies.

Prayer and the Curriculum

Whether seeking a classical education and a learned clergy, practical skills for evangelism and service, priestly formation, or some combination of these goals, seminary education has always been a conversation with the past centered in scripture.[17] Seminaries as residential schools were conceived as schools of piety formed by regular rounds of common worship. In addition to worship, in the classroom, in private devotions, or on retreat, scripture was read devotionally in the context of prayer. To use the language of spiritual exercises, the knowledge of God was grounded in practices of contemplation and examination. These spiritual exercises of the mind were shaped and informed by bodily spiritual exercises. Most significantly, residential seminary meant a certain withdrawal from the world and its daily demands to be formed as a more intentional community sharing a common life of prayer and meals and often also of service in the community beyond the seminary. Formation and learning were inseparable.

The historical, critical, comparative study of religion may be the great achievement of scholars and universities in the twentieth century. Such work moved the study of Christianity from narrow denominationalism and various forms of positivism (where truth is given as posited by some authority). Ecumenism increased, followed by inter-religious studies. Historical, critical perspectives, however, have also shaped theological disciplines as disciplines by divorcing them from spiritual disciplines. Such a divorce is reflected in the perceived distinction, if not opposition, between theory and practice.[18] Where faculty and student bodies are ecumenical, there is a broad, common, critical framework defining a field of study (such as biblical studies), but there is often a lack of understanding or comfort regarding different spiritual traditions and a desire not to impose particular forms of worship and spiritual practices. Common worship and more specific spiritual disciplines such as retreats, fasting, examination and individual or private confession of sins, spiritual direction, devotional reading, and meditation are increasingly voluntary, left to individual discretion. However, if the knowledge of God depends upon these spiritual exercises, then seminaries must reclaim a new asceticism as integral to their curriculum.

The rise of spirituality and the study of the spiritual—often as elective courses—are no substitutes for the integration of spiritual practices within the ongoing life of the seminary, beginning with common worship, the reading of scripture (as in *lectio divina*) and prayer.[19] Courses would also be taught differently. Biblical studies would not have a singular or narrow focus on historical critical analysis of the text, its setting, and its editing. Nor would biblical studies have a singular or narrow focus on the theology of a biblical writer. Instead, biblical studies would take time for reading the text. How different a class would be when begun and concluded with a reading of scripture, informed by critical, historical, and theological analysis, but left open, broken open, for contemplation or placed in conversation with the question of what is the Word of God that might be preached at this time and in this place. Similarly, a class in theology might include meditation on divine names or the meaning of glory.

Beyond the classroom, to place spiritual practices at the heart of theological education requires attention to the ordering of daily life. A policy addressing such matters as how connected we should be through cell phones and online computers may be excessively bureaucratic, if not autocratic. However, raising such matters that need to be addressed and establishing some guidelines for a rule of life are surely in order. Certainly common worship should be expected. Those who have never taken a retreat should do so. Practice in the contemplation of scripture is essential. Examining oneself and the heart's desire must not be avoided. At the least there is the need to discuss with students the disciplines of the spiritual life and to help them to set goals that will broaden and deepen their knowledge of God. This may be done with a spiritual director; however, too often provisions for spiritual direction (including the requirement to have a spiritual director) lead to segmenting spiritual exercises from the work of the faculty in general. The explicit curriculum of coursework competes with spiritual disciplines. The implicit curriculum suggests that academic studies are valued and spiritual disciplines are secondary and optional.

Episcopal seminaries in general and Virginia Theological Seminary in particular have a long tradition of spiritual disciplines centered in common worship. At Virginia Seminary such formation is often referred to a bit casually as "go to worship, go to class, go to lunch." Continued and explicit attention to spiritual formation is needed and specifically to spiritual exercises of both the mind and the body. The challenge is that there is no simple and uniform solution to establishing spiritual exercises and integrating them with critical theological studies, especially given the diversity of seminary students. If, however, seminaries are to deepen the knowledge of God and prepare persons to lead others into a deeper knowledge of God, they must explicitly address spiritual formation and assess students in terms of their attention and development of spiritual disciplines. This need not lead to an assessment of spiritual maturity. Rather, the need is to ensure that students attend to these matters, including setting goals regarding what they will do as matters of spiritual disciplines addressing mind and body. This can only be successful where seminaries ensure sufficient space to exercise spiritual disciplines and make these explicit and integral to the curriculum as a whole. After all, and most importantly in preparing persons for leadership in the Church as priest and pastors, as educators and evangelists, only the one who prays has knowledge of God.

Notes

1   Evagrius Ponticus, *Treatise on Prayer*, 61.

2   Aidan Kavanagh, *On Liturgical Theology* (New York: Pueblo, 1984), viii, 91–95.

3   See Michael Polanyi, *Personal Knowledge* (London: Routledge & K. Paul, 1958).

4   H. Richard Niebuhr, *Faith on Earth* (New Haven, CT: Yale, 1989), 67.

5   There is a significant literature developing such an integrated understanding of theology and spiritual exercises. See, for example, Mark McIntosh, *Divine Teaching: An Introduction to Christian Theology* (Blackwell, 2007). For an earlier development of the account given here, see Timothy F. Sedgwick, *The Christian Moral Life* (New York: Seabury, 2nd ed., 2008), 103–26.

6   Pierre Hadot, *Philosophy as a Way of Life*, tr. Michael Chase (Oxford: Blackwell, 1995), 1–109.

7   See Edmund Husserl, *Cartesian Meditation: An Introduction to Phenomenology*, tr. Dorion Cairns (The Hague: Martinus. Nijhoff, 1960), and Alfred Schutz, "Symbol, Reality and Society," *Collected Papers* I, ed. Maurice Natanson (The Hague: Martinus Nijhoff, 1970), 294–300.

8   Jacques Derrida, *The Gift of Death*, tr. David Wills (Chicago: University of Chicago Press, 1995), 101–09.

9   Augustine, *Confessions*, tr. Henry Chadwick (Oxford: Oxford University Press, 1991), Bk. II.iv-x (9–18, 28–34, 18).

10 For a classic statement of this method of correlation as integral to theological understanding, see David Tracy, *Blessed Rage for Order* (New York: Seabury, 1975).

11 Bamberger, *The Praktikos: Chapters on Prayer #60* (Kalamazoo, MI: Cistercian Publications, 1972), 65.

12 This phrase, drawn from the tradition of reflective philosophy represented by Gabriel Marcel, is from Margaret A. Farley, *Just Love: A Framework for Christian Sexual Ethics* (New York: Continuum, 2006), 116.

13 One of the first proposals for a new asceticism was Richard J. Foster, *Celebration of Discipline* (San Francisco: Harper & Row, 1978); more recently, see Dorothy Bass, *Practicing Our Faith* (San Francisco: Jossey-Bass, 1997).

14 The definition of sacrament as that which effects by signifying is from Thomas Aquinas. See Karl Rahner, "Introductory Observations on Thomas Aquinas' Theology of the Sacraments in General," *Theological Investigations*, vol. 14 (London: Darton, Longman, & Todd, 1976), 149–60.

15 For a recent account of embodiment in which she describes the human person as "embodied spirits, inspirited bodies," see Farley, *Just Love*, 116–32.

16 Dom Gregory Dix, *The Shape of the Liturgy* (London: Dacre, 1945); F.D. Maurice, *The Kingdom of Christ*, ed. Alec R. Vidler (London: SCM 1958; first published 1842); Charles Gore, *Belief in Christ* (New York: Scribner's, 1922); William Temple, *Christus Veritas* (London: Macmillan, 1924); Michael Ramsey, *The Gospel and the Catholic Church* (London: Longmans, Green and Co., 1936); Rowan Williams, *On Theology* (London: Blackwell, 2000); Sarah Coakley, *Powers and Submissions* (Oxford: Blackwell, 2002); Mark McIntosh, Divine Teaching.

17 See Charles R. Foster, Lisa Dahill, Lawrence Golemon, and Barbara Wang Tolentino, *Educating Clergy* (San Francisco, CA: The Carnegie Foundation, 2006), 190–223.

18 See, for example, Edward Farley, *Theologia: The Fragmentation and Unity of Theological Education* (Philadelphia: Fortress, 1983).

19 For a positive assessment of such a development see *Educating Clergy*, 258–60, 272–95.

Will We See the End of Common Prayer?

Robert W. Prichard

A ttending a worship service in an unfamiliar Episcopal congregation—particularly an urban one—in the early twenty-first century can be an experience that would tax even an experienced juggler. The visitor is often confronted with a prayer book, a multi-page bulletin, any number of handouts, and two or more hymnals. In addition there are mysterious extra books from which officiants read (the *Book of Occasional Services*, the four volumes of the *Enriching Our Worship* series, *Lesser Feasts and Fasts*, the *Altar Book*, the *Gospel Book*), and local conventions about whether or not members of the congregations actually follow the written texts that do appear in the Book of Common Prayer.

The situation is not unlike the description of the liturgical life of the medieval church offered more than fifty years ago by Episcopal liturgical scholar Massey Hamilton Shepherd, Jr. (1913–1990) in his commentary on the 1928 edition of the Book of Common Prayer. Shepherd explained the multiple books that had once been used in worship:

The liturgical books containing the formularies used in the service [of the medieval Catholic Church] were put together in such a way that all the parts needed by a single officiant were separated and gathered in one volume. Thus the celebrant had in his hands a Sacramentary, a book containing only the prayer that he himself said. The various chanters had their Antiphonaries, Responsorials, Graduals, Psalters, Hymnals; and the readers of the lessons their Lectionaries, Epistolaries, Evangeliaries, and so forth. To keep the entire service moving in its proper order and ceremony another officiant was required, who had in his Ordinary or Directory (commonly called the Pie in England) all the cues and rules of liturgical procedure.[1]

Shepherd did not, however, regard this multitude of books to be a good thing. On the contrary, he argued that one of the greatest gifts of the Anglican tradition was Thomas Cranmer's insight in offering a simple alternative to the complexity of worship books faced by English Christians before the Reformation.

For Shepherd, the creation of a simple liturgical resource was one of the two basic principles behind Thomas Cranmer's creation of the first two prayer books (1549 and 1552). Shepherd wrote that

The common prayer of the Church was to be easily manageable and readily understood by all the people, clergy and laity, learned and unlearned. The rites of the Church were so simplified that they could all be included in the cover of one book; and this book, with the Bible, would furnish all that was necessary for the celebration of the liturgy. Incidentally, this was a great savings in cost, and furthermore it meant that the entire liturgy of the Church could ultimately be placed in the hands of all of the people.[2]

Shepherd listed this principle first, ahead of what he regarded to be Cranmer's second principle—use of scripture. For Shepherd and for a generation of Episcopalians who read his works, the simplicity of a single basic volume of *common* prayer was basic to the Anglican tradition of worship.

Early twenty-first-century Episcopalians seem, however, to be moving in a very different direction. Indeed, some have moved beyond the desire for multiple supplementary volumes to question whether there is the need for any rite that is common to the whole Episcopal Church. Perhaps, some contemporary Episcopalians argue, what is needed is a collection of multiple resources from which individual celebrants and congregations might choose.

In 1997 the Episcopal Church's Church Publishing Company took a step in the direction of providing resources for such an approach by introducing the *Rite Brain*, the first in a series of CD volumes containing liturgical and musical resources. The Rite series promotional material explains that those who plan liturgy "no longer have to remember hundreds of details and rubrics to create interesting and varied liturgies" and are able easily to "customize each order of service."[3]

Clayton Morris, who is the former liturgical officer of the Episcopal Church, summed up this vision of an Episcopal Church without a single prayer book in a 1996 article. He suggested that "a growing library [of resources], with provision for adding new materials as they are developed" would serve the Episcopal Church better than a single book.[4] Before rushing to embrace this option, it may be useful, however, to consider the rationale that earlier generations of Episcopalians offered for the existence of a one-volume fixed liturgy. Before doing so, we will first consider a preliminary question about the meaning of liturgy.

Truth and Liturgy

On what basis do Christians make truth claims about the liturgy?" One might rephrase the question in more vernacular speech: Why bother with liturgy at all? Does it tell us anything that isn't already completely obvious? This question is tied to the broader question about the human capacity to have knowledge of God. How do we know about God? Contemporary Christians generally approach the question of the knowledge of God through one of two routes, each of which entails several variants.

The first route, explored by Friedrich Schleiermacher (1768–1834), Samuel Taylor Coleridge (1772–1834), and other Romantic theologians and philosophers of the nineteenth century, involves an expanded claim about human cognition. Human beings, such authors argued, have a capacity to experience God that somehow lies beyond the mere data collection of the five senses.[5] Coleridge called this capacity Reason and distinguished it from what he called Understanding (his term for data from the five senses and conclusions based upon it). He believed that Reason enabled human beings to experience truth and ultimately reality.

Schleiermacher and Coleridge understood the experience of ultimate reality in different ways. For Schleiermacher the experience was "a revelation of the Infinite in the finite."[6] The finite human who had this experience became aware of his or her dependence upon the infinite God. Thus, for Schleiermacher, "the common element in all those determinations of self-consciousness which predominantly express a receptivity affected from some outside quarter is the feeling of Dependence [German *Gefühl*]."[7] Coleridge, in contrast, explained the experience of ultimate reality in terms of the exercise of the imagination, particularly through the arts.

Some authors have found this expanded understanding of Reason to be very useful in talking about liturgy. Those taking such an approach understand prayer as the means by which human beings come into contact with God. This insight can be developed in several ways.

One alternative is to follow such Episcopal authors as Morton Kelsey and Urban T. Holmes in combining the insights of Coleridge and Schleiermacher with the work on the unconscious of Swiss psychologist Carl Jung (1875–1961).

According to this perspective, prayer is an imaginative activity by which the individual accesses basic subconscious archetypes, which in turn point to God. Thus Holmes, who was dean of the School of Theology of the University of the South at Sewanee, Tennessee, up to the time of his death, wrote in *Ministry and the Imagination* (1976) that "if the church is to be open to the presence of God in Christ now, it has to live a life of imagination." For him Jung provided a fruitful approach by teaching that it is in "the deep content of the unconscious ... [that] man begins to see the vision of God for his creation."[8] William Countryman (b. 1941) of the Church Divinity School of the Pacific has developed similar themes in his *Living on the Border of the Holy* (1999).[9]

Another variant of the claim about prayer is built upon aesthetics. One can focus on the parallel between being moved by great works of music or art and experiencing the holy through the liturgy. F. H. Brabant, author of the initial essay in *Liturgy and Worship* (1950), identified worship as "religious drama, a full expression and satisfaction of the aesthetic instincts." But, he wrote, worship "is far more than a pageant stimulating our instincts of appreciation, or a presentation under symbolic forms of an ideal which ought to be true. It is ... a way by which the soul passes up to the highest reality."[10] Even more than good art and music, the liturgy moves our hearts to the contemplation and knowledge of God.

A second explanation for our knowledge of God and ultimate reality is dependent in part on the insights of Ludwig Wittgenstein (1889–1951) and other linguistic philosophers, and upon the insistence of theologian Karl Barth (1886–1968) that the task of theology is to bring consistency to the language of the Church. According to those who take this approach, there is something about language that reveals deeper realities.

This linguistic insight can be developed in a variety of very different ways. For some, language is important because of its content.[11] In religious terms, language can be the vehicle by which truth imparted by Christ to the disciples (and discerned at other moments in the history of the Church) is passed on to contemporary worshipers. The liturgy, like the Bible, is one of the chief forms in which this content is passed on. This is the approach to the liturgy taken by the ecumenical statement titled *Baptism, Eucharist, and Ministry*. The document identified worship as part of an apostolic tradition of "continuity in faith, worship and mission."[12] From this perspective the truth in liturgy is dependent upon its ability to preserve revealed truth over time and upon our ability to interpret and understand that truth.

It is also possible to suggest that language itself or some linguistic construction, such as metaphor, is revelatory. Lutheran liturgical theologian Gordon Lathrop and feminist theologian Sallie McFague take this approach. McFague suggests that "a metaphor expresses [what] cannot be said directly or apart from it, for if it could be, one would have said it directly. Here, metaphor is a strategy of desperation, not decoration; it is an attempt to speak about what we do not know in terms of what we do know."[13] Lathrop paraphrases this definition and applies it specifically to the liturgy. A metaphor is, he says, "the application of the wrong name to something in order to reveal a thing that could not otherwise be spoken."[14] He then argues that the basic structure of the liturgy functions in a manner parallel to metaphor. The liturgy is a series of "juxtapositions," a set of tensions that reveal things about the Christian faith that could not be spoken of in other terms.[15] "For Christians," he writes, "all texts and all rituals are wrong words. All have to be broken to speak the Christian faith, the resurrection, the encounter with God in the crucified Jesus, the new vision of the world."[16] The juxtapositions in the liturgy open to the worshiper a new vision of the world.

Yet another way to develop the insight about language is to draw upon the work of Claude Lévi-Strauss (1908–2009) and other structuralists, who question whether any objective or permanent reality lies behind language. Language is a social construct in which dominant social classes and groups impose their vision of reality on others. An investigation into language is fruitful, nonetheless, for it reveals a great deal about human institutions and culture. This approach provides a useful tool for critics of the liturgy.

Feminist liturgical scholars, for example, often draw on this understanding of language, suggesting that traditional liturgies have been shaped by male, hierarchical exercise of power and are in need of reform. Marjorie Proctor-Smith, who teaches at Perkins School of Theology at Southern Methodist University, wrote in *Praying with Our Eyes Open* (1995) that "patriarchal discourse is hierarchic, dualistic discourse" in which "everything can be accounted for in two categories of existence: the dominant category and then everything else," which is then understood to be heresy. This approach, she suggests, identifies women "with heresy and heterodoxy," and regards them as "weak and thus subject to the temptations of heretical thinking and behavior."[17] The liturgy, she argues, is a mechanism by which men control women: "Liturgically speaking, this striving for unity and for control of women can be seen in . . . defenses of 'true' worship by means of the creation or defense of 'official' fixed liturgical texts."[18] The role of the liturgical reformer is then to right this imbalance in the text.

Liturgical scholars, then, take a variety of different positions on the relationship of the liturgy to truth. For some, prayer is the language of an extra-sensory communication with ultimate reality, known through digging deep into the basic archetypes of the human consciousness or by a rising on high with the contemplation of the beautiful and true. For others language is a code by which truth is handed on, new meaning is revealed, or social dominance is maintained. Many who write about the liturgy either assume, without explicitly identifying, one of these approaches or draw upon several of them.

A Rationale for
Fixed Forms of Worship

Does a fixed liturgy have any place amidst such competing claims for the relationship of liturgy to truth? Some would argue that a fixed liturgy is important precisely because of such claims.

More than a century ago, a number of rather astute German philosophers, including Ludwig Feuerbach (1804–1872) and Frederich Nietzsche (1844–1900), pointed out the human capacity to remake God in one's own image. Humans attribute to God, they argued, the characteristics that they see as ideal in themselves. Neither of the two broad strategies discussed in the previous section for claiming truth in liturgy is immune to this danger of self-delusion. One may seek to plumb the depths of the human consciousness in search of basic archetypes, only to find shallow rationalizations for one's own prejudices. One may look for meaning in language, while in fact using language to impose one's own perspectives on others.

Previous generations of Episcopalians have generally argued, nonetheless, that the use of fixed forms of worship can be a powerful and important resource in the struggle to confront the danger of self-deception. Public use of forms of prayer composed over time by a diverse group of individuals, passed on and identified as authoritative by others in different cultural situations, and then received and used by the present generation provide a counterbalance to personal and even societal self-interest. Massey Shepherd, Jr. explained, for example, that "the very purpose of liturgy is to recall to us and revive in us what we should pray for and how we should pray." Writing in the years after World War II, he went on to ask:

> How far would our intercessions reach beyond the
> circle of our immediate preoccupations without
> a guide, such as, for example, the Litany? Would
> we, in these days, be so ready to pray, 'that it may

please thee to forgive our enemies, persecutors, and slanderers, and to turn their hearts?' ... The liturgy crystallizes the experience of the whole Church. It is the common vocabulary of the 'communion of the saints' both in time and space. We are made aware of needs, of truths, of aspirations beyond the capacity of any single individual to imagine, however gifted or spiritually minded. [19]

The British apologist C.S. Lewis (1898–1963) made a similar argument about the use of a fixed system of lessons in a liturgy. In his *Screwtape Letters*, Lewis drew a sharp contrast between the preacher who followed the lectionary and the cleric who simply followed the dictates of his own heart. The *Screwtape Letters* were a fictional correspondence between two devils about the best way to tempt a human being, referred to as the patient. Screwtape advises Wormwood on his patient's choice of churches:

> The two churches nearest to him, I have looked up in the office. Both have certain claims. At the first of these the vicar is a man who has been so long engaged in watering down the faith to make it easier for a supposedly incredulous and hardheaded congregation that it is now he who shocks his parishioners with his unbelief, not vice versa. He has undermined many a soul's Christianity. His conduct of the services is also admirable. In order to spare the laity all 'difficulties' he has deserted both the lectionary and the appointed psalms and now, without noticing it, revolves round the little treadmill of his fifteen favorite psalms and twenty favorite lessons. We are thus safe from the dangers that any truth not already familiar to him and to his flock should ever reach them through Scripture. [20]

Lewis agrees that one of the chief advantages of a fixed liturgy is that it enlarges our own small vision of God and forces us to recognize and respond to a much broader vision of God's initiative in human life. One needs to proceed with caution before accepting any liturgical solution that leaves the entire shape of the liturgy in the hands of a single celebrant. The church would not be well served by being insulated from "any truth that is not already familiar."

Notes

1   Massey Hamilton Shepherd, Jr., *The Oxford American Prayer Book Commentary* (New York: Oxford University Press, 1950), xii–xiii.

2   Massey H. Shepherd, Jr., *The Worship of the Church*, vol. 4 of the Church's Teaching Series (Greenwich, CT: Seabury Press, 1952), 87–88.

3   Church Publishing: Bookstore, "The Rite Stuff, a Liturgical Planning Resource for the Episcopal Church," <http://www.churchpublishing.org/index.cfm?fuseaction=product&ProductID=251> (accessed 5 August 2004).

4   Clayton L. Morris, "Prayer Book Revision or Liturgical Renewal? The Future of Liturgical Text" in *A Prayer Book for the 21st Century*, ed. Ruth Meyers, Liturgical Studies 3 (New York: Church Hymnal, 1996), 250.

5   This claim to data that was not tied to five senses was, in part, an attempt to respond to the persuasive arguments of eighteenth-century philosopher Immanuel Kant (1724–1804). In his *Critique of Pure Reason* Kant had questioned the ability of human senses to provide any true knowledge about God.

6   Friedrich Schleiermacher, *On Religion: Speeches to Its Cultured Despisers*, trans. John Oman (New York: Harper & Row, Torchbooks, 1958), 36.

7   Friedrich Schleiermacher, *The Christian Faith*, 2 vols. (New York: Harper & Row, Torchbooks, 1963) 1:12–13.

8   Urban T. Holmes III, *Ministry and the Imagination* (New York: Seabury, 1976), 88, 150.

9   Louis William Countryman, *Living on the Border of the Holy: Renewing the Priesthood of All* (Harrisburg: Morehouse, 1999).

10 Frank Herbert Brabant, "Worship in General" in *Liturgy and Worship, a Companion to the Prayer Books of the Anglican Communion*, ed. W. K. Lowther Clarke and Charles Harris (London: SPCK, 1950), 31, 34.

11 Hans Frei (1922–1988) and the advocates of the "Yale School" of theology would focus specially on narrative content. It is the recitation of the story of God's mighty acts that confronts, transforms, and inspires the Church.

12 *Baptism, Eucharist and Ministry*, Faith and Order Paper No. 111 (Geneva: World Council of Churches, 1982), 29.

13 Sallie McFague, *Models of God: Theology for an Ecological Nuclear Age* (Philadelphia: Fortress Press, 1987), 33.

14 Gordon Lathrop, *Holy People* (Minneapolis: Fortress, 1999), 86.

15 Gordon Lathrop, *Holy Things: A Liturgical Theology* (Minneapolis: Augsburg Fortress, 1993), 35, 48, 54.

16 Lathrop, *Holy Things* , 50.

17 Marjorie Proctor-Smith, *Praying with Our Eyes Open: Engendering Feminist Liturgical Prayer* (Nashville: Abingdon Press, 1995), 24.

18 Proctor-Smith, *Praying*, 26.

19 Massey Hamilton Shepherd, Jr., *The Living Liturgy* (New York: Oxford University Press, 1946), 9–10.

20 C. S. Lewis, *The Screwtape Letters* (New York: MacMillan, 1980), 74–75.

Opening the Table

Stephen B. Edmondson

In January of 2006 I undertook a project exploring the practice of opening the eucharistic table—inviting forward all present, whether baptized or not, to receive the bread and wine of Christ's offer of himself—in conversation with four Episcopal churches that had embraced this practice. My goal was to provide a richer matrix of theological understanding for opening the table, and I pursued this goal out of the deep conviction that the theological understanding which I sought lay implicit within the practice of these congregations. I was relying on an understanding of liturgical theology as it is outlined by Aidan Kavanaugh. Our liturgy expresses a theology principally through the change that overtakes a Christian community when they are engaged by God in their liturgical practice; theology emerges in the conversion of the community through their liturgical encounter with God in Christ that the Eucharist enacts. Liturgical theology in a secondary sense would be analytical reflection on this conversion carried out in texts and conversations—reflections that seek to identify and understand the conversion that the liturgical encounter has catalyzed. The practice of opening the table, I surmised, was in the first place such a conversion of practicing Christian communities in their liturgical encounters with God, and the goal of my project would be to make explicit the theological underpinnings and manifestations of this change, so that the Church could learn to live more fully into the work which God had begun within it.

Through my work with these congregations, I was led to the parable of the lost son as the central theological metaphor through which this practice might be understood. In the parable, a man who has shamed his family, wasted his inheritance, and fallen into dissolution and despair returns home seeking only lowly employment and sustenance for the most basic needs of his life. He expects to find disapproval and judgment as well. But when he arrives, he is greeted instead by the loving exuberance of his father. This father, who stood looking for the return of this alienated son since his departure, runs to meet him and, embracing him, offers him both forgiveness and a feast for which the son never dared to hope. Indeed, the father clothes him and takes him to the table before he has even had the chance to bathe.

Christ's vision of God's compassionate care for humanity, expressed in this parable, is the vision that has inspired the Christian practice of opening the eucharistic table. This vision sees the world through the promise of God's love and forgiveness that lies at the heart of Christ's mission—a forgiveness that is given before it is asked and a love that seeks us out before we know that we are lost, embracing us as soon as we are within its reach. Opening the table incarnates this offer of love to a hungry world, fulfilling the baptismal ministry to which Christ has called the Church. At the invitation to the Eucharist at St. Bartholomew's Episcopal Church in San Diego, the celebrant proclaims, "All who seek God are welcome to the Lord's Table to receive the Bread and Wine. Even if you do not seek God, God seeks you. Come and hold in your hand and taste on your lips the love which we cannot comprehend."

The practice of opening the eucharistic table to all, regardless of their baptismal status, is a practice that has evolved among Christian churches in the last three decades, despite its not having been formally authorized by the Episcopal Church. It grew out of the ecumenical concern to open our tables to all Christians, and from this former practice churches were moved to ask how inclusively we should define the children of God for whom Christ has prepared this feast. Many churches have come to the answer that Christ's embrace—like the embrace of the Father in the parable—extends to all. The love of God that is offered in the Eucharist is not only free from constraint by differing Christian confessions (the impulse behind open communion), but is also free to extend itself to touch those who do not confess Christ. Inherent in this conclusion is a shift in the understanding of the Eucharist in line with the vision of the parable of the lost son. The Eucharist is God's feast, and God bestows this feast not on those who have made themselves acceptable to God, but on those whom God would draw into fullness of life with God, which is the promise of the feast. In reaching this conclusion, those who have opened the table recognize their place with the lost son, in humble gratitude for God's extravagant, ever-beckoning, ever-revealing love. Through our participation in the Eucharist, we are all learning how to feast with God.

This vision of the kingdom feast that we celebrate weekly in our churches is coherent with what I learned about a communal practice of the kingdom under Martha Horne—it is a practice that sets hospitality at the center of the Christian life, but that understands hospitality in a way that is thoroughly scriptural and evangelical. It is a hospitality grounded in the discomfiting good news of the Gospel of Jesus.

The latter aspect of my conviction, however—that this practice not only deals with hospitality, but that it also is a thoroughly scriptural practice—needs further exploration and explanation. The newness of the contemporary practice of opening the table has left the scriptural basis for the practice underdeveloped. In this essay, therefore, I will consider one dimension of this scriptural basis—the rootedness of this practice in Jesus' table ministry—but I need to be clear at the outset that I take up Jesus' table ministry not as the center of the practice's scriptural context, but only as one aspect of a broader understanding.

Any scriptural understanding of the Church's eucharistic practice must center itself where both the Gospels and the eucharistic liturgy point us, on the story of Jesus' last supper with his disciples. But this last supper, in turn, invokes at least three broader contexts for its understanding: the Passover tradition within the Hebrew Scriptures, the tradition of the Kingdom feast, evoked in these same scriptures and carried throughout Jesus' preaching, and Jesus' table ministry with tax collectors, sinners, disciples, scribes, and Pharisees. I will elsewhere explore more fully this broader complex, but in this article I wish to take up the one aspect, Jesus' table ministry, that expands on the central theological vision implicit within this practice—the parable of the lost son that I introduced above.

There has been a tendency among both opponents and proponents of opening the table to break Jesus' table ministry apart from his last supper with his disciples, but the four canonical gospels indicate that they are to be held together. At his last supper with his disciples, I would argue, Jesus lifts up the activity of breaking bread at table as the center of his life and ministry, so that his disciples are to "do this to remember him." My task here, therefore, is to explore what Jesus did in his ministry of table fellowship that forms, by his command, the center of our memory of him.

My exploration will be rooted in an extended reading of Luke's gospel, since Luke most explicitly holds together Jesus' breaking of bread at his last supper with the broader run of his table fellowship, which forms the substance of ministry. Luke's gospel is, in the first place, a story of table fellowship. Throughout the gospel, it has been commented, Jesus is either at a meal, going to a meal, or coming from a meal.[1] For Luke, you cannot properly remember Jesus apart from these meals and what he says about them. But Luke also holds this broader fellowship closely with Jesus' last supper with his disciples. Indeed, in Luke, Jesus' fourfold act of breaking bread at table (taking, blessing, breaking, and giving), which centers the last supper narrative, also structures his gospel as a whole. In Luke, we find Jesus taking, blessing, breaking, and giving bread not only at the last supper, but also at the feeding of the five thousand—after which he turns from his ministry in Galilee to head towards Jerusalem and the cross—and with the two disciples on the road to Emmaus, where he reveals both the meaning of his death and ministry and the truth of his resurrection. By placing Jesus' breaking of the bread at the three nodal points in his narrative—Jesus' culmination of his Galilean ministry, his embrace of the cross, and his revelation of himself in his resurrection—Luke is demanding that we understand Jesus through this action, but he is also suggesting that we understand this action through the broader narrative of table fellowship which forms the substance of his text. Let's explore this intuition further to see what it yields.

Table Fellowship

Luke's gospel is a story of table fellowship. It is a story that revolves around meals and stories of meals, and we must understand that that these meals are not simply about food, but about the fellowship transacted through them; hence, the emphasis on table fellowship. It's not that food isn't important in these stories of meals—what makes a shared meal significant in the first place is the sharing and consumption of the stuff of life. We don't understand the story of the feeding of the five thousand at all if we don't get that Jesus feeds a hungry multitude. Food, in this story, is the gift, while also serving as a metaphor for God's greater gift. We don't live by bread alone, but we don't live without bread, either.

Food is significant in relationship to these stories of meals, however, not only as that which nourishes our bodies, but also as that around which we gather our communities. We build our social relationships through food and the offer of food, and life depends upon these relationships as much as it does the food that we are offered through them. Food is significant, then, for the fellowship that it constitutes. Within the context of the biblical story, there is a holiness to food, as the stuff of life given to us by God, that sanctifies the relationships through which food is shared and consumed. This holiness is evident in the mandate of hospitality. Abraham shares food with three travelers, and entertains angels unawares. He establishes relationship with these strangers through his offer of food, while God establishes relationship with him likewise through his hospitality. Through his offer of food, Abraham has fellowship with God.

Anthropologists have long noted the capacity for the sharing of food to define social relationships. To know who shares food with whom in a society is to have a social map of that society, insofar as this sharing of food initiates "an interconnected complex of mutuality and reciprocity."[2] In Jesus' Jewish milieu, this capacity of food-sharing to define social relationships was heightened by its theological dimension. Jewish meals always begin with a blessing—"Blessed be thou, O Lord our God, eternal King, who bringest forth bread from the earth." This divine invocation acknowledges that the web of relationship that the meal always enacts is already grounded in the relationship of the participants with God, who provides the meal and is the ultimate host. Thus, Gillian Feeley-Harnik argues that every Jewish meal is in some sense a covenant meal—a meal of the community who have bound themselves to one another through their mutual belonging to or being fed by God.[3] This covenantal sense of the meal was strengthened in the years following the Babylonian captivity of the Jews, when a heightened awareness emerged of the power of purity laws surrounding their food to bind the Jewish people to one another, to mark them off as God's people in the midst of their enemies.

Meals, then, in Jesus' Jewish context, were occasions for establishing and celebrating both the boundaries around and

Staying One, Remaining Open

the relationships among God's people, as distinct from those outside of God's covenant—those who were impure, apostate, or who worshiped false gods. To break bread with another—and we must remember that blessing the bread was intrinsic to its breaking—was to proclaim God and to claim, with the other, fellowship with God through that action.

We can understand the gospel accounts of Jesus' meal ministry and what they tell us of Jesus only when we grasp this theological dimension to these meals. Some contemporary scholars have emphasized the social revolution that Jesus initiates through his willingness to eat with the outsiders: he subverted the class system, they claim, through which the powerful ordered society, and so he was a threat to the system and the power that it maintained.[4] What they miss is the dependence of this social revolution on an underlying religious revolution—that Jesus, in his meal ministry, challenged contemporary understandings of both the make-up of the people of God (those with whom God was in fellowship) and God's approach to those who stood outside this fellowship. Again, to break bread with someone in Jesus' context was to share fellowship with God.

Jesus' meal ministry, to return to the beginning of this article, needs to be understood through the lens of the parable of the prodigal. Certainly we understand the parable only as we see the shift in the relationship between the two brothers—a social revolution of a kind—but it's clear within the parable that this shift is driven by the revolution in relationship that needs to take place between each brother and the father. Indeed, if we read the parable with Jesus taking the part of the father, it is remarkable the insight that it offers to Jesus' meal ministry overall. In his meals with the tax collectors and sinners, we see the father's reception of the prodigal younger brother who returns to his father's house and embrace. In his meals with the religious authorities, we see the father's instruction of the elder brother of his misunderstanding of his relationship with both his father and the prodigal. In both cases, Jesus is seeking to reconcile God's lost children to the ways and fellowship of the Father. Indeed, we could argue that Jesus' practice of table fellowship was his own liturgy of reconciliation. This will be clearer if we look at his table fellowship in relation not only to the tax collectors and sinners and religious authorities, but also to his disciples, always with the template of the parable of the prodigal to guide us. Once we are clear on the dynamics of this table fellowship, we can turn to Jesus' eschatological teaching on this fellowship to develop more fully the theological dimension of Jesus' liturgy of reconciliation.

Jesus and the Younger Son

Perhaps the most notable and historically reliable aspect of Jesus' ministry was his table fellowship with tax collectors and sinners—the outcasts of the people of Israel. This practice earned him the title of a "drunkard and a glutton" from his enemies, which was, in some ways, to call him a prodigal son,[5] and it led to his rejection by the Jewish religious authorities, putting into motion the events that led to his crucifixion. It is clear from the gospel accounts that this was not an accidental practice of Jesus, but his intentional pursuit of outreach to the outcast of God's people—his attempt to draw them back within the healing embrace of God's tender care. When queried by the Pharisees about his practice of table fellowship with sinners, he responds "Those who are well have no need of a physician, but those who are sick; I have come to call not the righteous but sinners to repentance" (Luke 5:31–32). This ministry, in other words, was his embrace of the prodigal son, his liturgy of reconciliation.

Luke's stories of Jesus' table fellowship with sinners are various—the feast with Levi (5:27–38), John and Jesus, the Bridegroom and the Ascetic (7:18–35); the anointing of Jesus' feet (7:36–50); the Pharisees' complaints (15:1–2); and the meal with Zaccheus (19:1–10)—but they share three common elements of gift, call, and repentance. Discerning the variable relations among these three elements within these stories helps us to understand the dynamics of Jesus' liturgy of reconciliation. Indeed, within the stories, we will find these three elements ordered differently, but upon closer examination, we will find that the element of gift—Jesus' gift of himself in fellowship—underlies each story and the gospel narrative as a whole.

We can begin to uncover the relationship of gift, call, and repentance if we look at two stories that bracket Christ's meal ministry—the call of Levi at the beginning and the call of Zaccheus at the end, stories which reveal the dynamics of these elements in their interactions with one another. Both stories are fairly simple. In the first, Christ has set out on his ministry, calling the people to repentance and belief in the Kingdom, and he sees Levi, the tax collector (who, as a tax collector, would be a notorious sinner). He calls Levi to follow him, and Levi leaves everything. We immediately find Jesus at a feast at Levi's house, surrounded by tax collectors and other sinners. Here the Pharisees ask him how he can dine with sinners, and he responds with the above quotation about his mission to sinners. In the story of Zaccheus, Jesus sees Zaccheus (a chief tax collector, or a king among sinners) in a tree and orders him down to play the host to Jesus. Again, there is grumbling about Jesus' fellowship with sinners. Zaccheus responds to Jesus' presence at his table by repenting of crimes against his people and promising restitution. Jesus declares that Zaccheus, a son of Abraham, has found salvation and reminds everyone of his own mission, still, to the sinful.

The dynamics of both stories are fairly straightforward. In the story of Levi, Jesus issues a call—to come follow him. Given the context of the story—Jesus' proclamation of repentance and the Kingdom—we can assume that this proclamation was implicit in the call, so that Levi's response included both. By leaving everything to follow Jesus, he is repenting of life in opposition to God's people (which was the reality of being a tax collector) and not only believing in Christ's good news, but joining himself to it. We can imagine that he did not yet understand to what he had joined himself. Finally, Christ bestows himself as a gift to Levi and to the sinners who surrounded them, sitting at table with them in fellowship at a feast. It is a story of call, repentance, and gift. In the story of Zaccheus, we find these elements ordered differently. Jesus calls Zaccheus to come down, so that he can offer him his gift of fellowship. Zaccheus responds to this call and gift by first preparing a place for Jesus at table, and then by repenting, seemingly in response to those who question Jesus' gift of himself to the sinful.

Both stories, then, begin with a call, but in one case, it is a call to repentance and commitment to the Kingdom, while in the other it is the call to receive the gift of Christ's presence. Both stories, likewise, involve repentance, but in each the repentance is differently positioned, in one case preceding and in the other following the gift. Christ's gift of himself is positioned differently in the story, as well, but this gift, nonetheless, stands at the center of each story. This is evident within the stories insofar as the gift is the center of the controversy generated by the call, the gift, and the repentance. In both stories, it is Jesus' willingness to sit at table with sinners that evokes the anger of the Pharisees. But the centrality of the gift in these stories is more evident if we turn to a third story of fellowship that is only about gift. When Jesus is invited to dine with Simon the Pharisee, a notoriously sinful woman comes to wash his feet with her tears and anoint them with oil. Christ's willingness to allow this to happen—his gift of himself in receiving her love—arouses the ire of table companions, as we would guess. In this story, Jesus' willingness to receive the woman's love is the whole of the action. There is no call, and though we might imagine that repentance was attached to the forgiveness by God that provoked her love, neither of these is anywhere noted. Again, the story is simply about Christ's gift of himself and the admittance of this woman, who is marked by her great love, into God's Kingdom.

What do I mean, however, in terming Jesus' table fellowship in these stories as his gift of himself? I can clarify this if we return to the story of Levi for a deeper look at this gift. As we have observed already, Jesus' simple bestowal of fellowship in the story is a gift, since he declares his solidarity with his tablemates through this fellowship. And given that Jesus is a respected religious teacher (Jesus was respected, at least by the people) and that he bestows his fellowship on the religiously outcast, he is bestowing the further gift of fellowship among the people of God. In the story immediately following the story of Levi, moreover, the Pharisees wonder why there is such feasting among Jesus and his disciples, and Jesus replies that when the bridegroom is present, only a feast is appropriate. Jesus' presence at the table with the outcast, then, bestows upon them not only fellowship with the people of God, but a place at the table in the feast of the bridegroom—a place at the Kingdom feast, if you will. In this way, finally, Jesus' table fellowship embodies the good news to which he called Levi and to which Levi responded. Jesus, in other words, does not simply proclaim that the Kingdom of God is at hand, but through his presence, as the bridegroom at table with those who have embraced this Kingdom gospel, he turns their meal into a Kingdom feast.

This final theme of embodiment is central to understanding Jesus' ministry and proclamation of the Kingdom. In the story immediately preceding the feast with Levi, a paralytic is brought to Jesus, and Jesus pronounces his sins forgiven. When his authority to forgive sins is questioned, he manifests that authority through its embodiment in the healing of the man's paralysis. Jesus here doesn't simply preach the Kingdom where the broken are healed; he realizes it, both spiritually and bodily. So too in his table fellowship. There he doesn't merely teach about the feast of the Kingdom, but he embodies it through his presence. Here the gift is not the healing of another's body, but the gift of his own, there at table. And he truly is offering his body there, since this gift of himself at table leads him to the cross and his death for these outcast whom he has reconciled with God. When Jesus, therefore, explains in this story that he comes as a physician to heal the sinful, we must see that his fellowship, his presence, his body is the medicine that he offers to enable this reconciliation. This is why I term it a liturgy of reconciliation.

Placing this emphasis on Christ's gift of himself in his ministry to the outcast—to the younger son of the parable—does not devalue repentance in these stories. It only recognizes that repentance here is dependent upon the gift; it is located in an orbit around the gift. Jesus' teaching on his ministry of reconciliation in the fifteenth chapter of Luke makes this more evident. This is the chapter where we find the parable of the lost son, but this parable is preceded by two others—the story of the man who seeks his lost sheep and the woman who seeks her lost coin. In both stories, it is the seeking after the lost and the joy in response to their recovery that is emphasized. The repentance of the sheep or the coin has no place in either story; indeed, it makes no sense even to wonder at its place. These two parables, then, form the context for our understanding of the parable of the prodigal and shape our understanding of seeking and repentance within it.

Interpreters often describe the central action of the parable of the lost son as the repentance of the younger son and the gracious reception of that repentance by the father, who embraces the son once the son has realized his folly. This interpretation of the parable makes little sense on at least two levels. First, it belies the context of the parable in its relation to the parables of the lost sheep and coin. If we are to understand these parables in parallel, then this reading of the prodigal would suggest that the first two parables should emphasize the effort of the sheep and the coin to return themselves to their owners, while the owner's joy would center on his or her good fortune at owning such a well-oriented sheep. But that is not where the weight of any of these parables lies. Just as with the parables of the lost sheep and coin the emphasis lay on the diligent care of the shepherd and housewife seeking out their beloved, so in the parable of the prodigal, the central dynamic is the searching, embracing love of the father who brings the lost son back into the family. It is the father's gift of his embrace that drives the story.

Moreover, we haven't understood the parable of the prodigal until we grasp the ambiguity of the son's so-called repentance that leads him to return home. Luke gives us several signals that we should look at this repentance with a cynical eye, all of them related to calculation behind the actions of the son. We first need to note that the son's repentance is formulated in what we might call "self-talk"—the son "came to himself and said . . . ." Within Luke's gospel there are four other similar formulations of self-talk—the rich man who counsels himself to build great barns to hold his harvest, the unjust steward who counsels himself to defraud his master of contractual value to make friends for himself when he is dismissed, the unjust judge who decides to settle the widow's claim to buy himself some peace, and the arrogant Pharisee who confides to himself in prayer that he is better than the near-by publican. Self-talk, in other words, is not the mark of sincerity or integrity in Luke's gospel. Admittedly, in the parable of the prodigal, we could read that he "came to himself and said . . . " simply as "he came to his senses" and dismiss these other parallels. Further examination, however, suggests that we should not dismiss this connection so simply, for the younger son's conversation with himself resembles the conversations of the rich man, the unjust steward, the unjust judge, and the self-righteous Pharisee more than it does the uncalculated self-abasement of the publican— it is calculating, aimed at material gain, and shows little or no sorrow for the harm that he has caused others. The father in the parable dismisses this so-called repentance, moreover, cutting off the son before he has even finished his well-rehearsed production.

Again, I am not arguing for a devaluation of repentance either in this parable or in Jesus' ministry as a whole. The parables of chapter 15 are told, after all, in response to pharisaical critique of Jesus' table fellowship with tax collectors and sinners who were coming to him—who were responding to his preaching—and this fits the emphasis on repentance that is a distinctive mark of Luke's gospel.[6] Rather, I am simply pointing out the inherent incompleteness and ambiguity of all repentance. Repentance is essential to the reconciliation that Jesus effects between God and God's people, but it is understood rightly only in its essential relationship to Christ's gift of himself. There was no reconciliation between the younger son and the father if the younger son did not return home, whatever his motives. But his life changes truly only upon his return, when he is embraced by the father and recognizes that home represents not economic sustenance or benefit (his attitude on his first leaving and his return), but the enveloping love of the father. Those tax collectors and sinners who gathered at table with Jesus could gather there only through some modicum of repentance. They required a desire to share table with the man of God. But their true repentance was possible only upon their reception of the gift of Jesus, which means that their repentance grew and deepened as they came to a deeper understanding and reception of this one who sat at table with them. This, indeed, is the heart of Jesus' call to repentance. The Kingdom of God is near—the Kingdom that was embodied in his table fellowship with sinners—repent in response to this Kingdom which has embraced you and believe the good news that you experience.

Jesus and the Elder Son

Similar dynamics of call, gift, and repentance are evident in Jesus' meals with the religious authorities in Luke. Here, again, we find Jesus dining with sinners, but in this case the sin has an entirely different texture. It is the sin of the elder brother, who does not understand the love of the father or the nature of his fellowship, so that he rejects not only his younger brother, but the father's love, as well. With this latter rejection, he, like the younger brother, has rejected the father. This is the case of the Pharisees and the scribes, as Luke depicts them. They have not only rejected the outcast of Israel—their brothers and sisters—but they also reject the in-breaking of God's Kingdom, of God's love, in God's embrace of these outcast through Jesus' table liturgy of reconciliation.

In response to their rejection of God's love for the outcast, Jesus responds in a way similar to the father in the parable—not by banishing them, but by reaching out to them in love, as well. Jesus offers himself to them in table fellowship—an offer of self that, again, will be fulfilled when they take him to Pilate to be crucified. Just as we must regard these religious authorities as sinners like those with whom Jesus dined throughout Luke, so we must understand Jesus' willingness to sit at table with them as a piece of his broader practice of table fellowship. With this gift of himself at table came the consistent call to recognize the Kingdom, to embrace the Father's love for the younger son, to accept Jesus and his ministry to the outcast. It was a call to repent from their ways of exclusion, arrogance, and inattention to God's mission of love and to join themselves to the feast which God was hosting in and through Jesus. Gift, call, and in response, there was no repentance, at least as recorded by Luke. (We should note that John does record one Pharisee, Nicodemus, who is at least open to Jesus' call.) This lack of repentance does not break our pattern of the dynamic of Jesus' table fellowship, for one point of the stories of Jesus' meals with Pharisees is their refusal to repent. Repentance, in other words, is present in these stories in its absence.

What would a proper response to Jesus' call to the religious authorities have looked like? What would it mean to fulfill the call of the elder son? I argue elsewhere that Jesus is the preeminent fulfillment of this call. He is the one who, sharing everything with the father, joins himself to the father's seeking love for the lost and pursues them even into the far country where he can offer them the father's loving embrace. Here I want to build on this suggestion and argue that in his instructions to his disciples to follow after his example, Jesus articulates the proper response of the elder son that he, himself, embodied. The father in the parable called on the son to come to share in his brother's return and reconciliation—his rebirth. An elder brother who was truly caught up in the spirit of the father's love would not have simply joined in this celebration, but would have led in the preparations, even serving at the table.

Across the gospels, Jesus is found teaching the disciples that they are to pattern their lives after his. They are called not to lord their authority, as his close followers, over those entrusted to their care. Rather, they are to serve, even as he served. In each of the synoptic gospels, Jesus instructs his disciples on this matter in response to an argument among them over who is the greatest (Matthew 20:25–28; Mark 10:42–45; Luke 22:24–30). Luke's gospel, however, is unique in placing this pericope after a meal or, to be more specific, after the meal of Jesus' last supper with them. This redaction of the story transforms Jesus' instruction of his disciples to be servants into a more specific call to serve at table, as Jesus has served the outcast at table throughout his ministry. They, in other words, are not only to accept the in-breaking of God's Kingdom through Jesus' table fellowship with the outcast, but are also to embrace and further that in-breaking by making Jesus' ministry their own.

Luke's placement of these instructions to serve after the last supper entails a second implication beyond the call to serve at table. They also help to solidify an understanding of this last supper with the whole of Jesus' table ministry—the argument which we are presently exploring. It would be difficult to make the claim that Jesus, in this meal, is calling on his disciples to set themselves apart from the unwashed in a manner like unto the Pharisees when they are to dine together, given his immediate instruction to serve at table—to join him in his table fellowship with the outcast. We see this point even more clearly if we turn to the one meal with the multitude where Luke wants us to see a specific parallel with the Last Supper, that is, the feeding of the five thousand.

In this meal, we see the disciples taking up the role that

Jesus has commended to them, as they serve the gathered multitude with the bread that Jesus has blessed and broken. Given Luke's explicit signal of the eucharistic overtones of this meal—Jesus here takes, blesses, breaks and gives the bread as he does at his last supper with his disciples—we cannot help but to read this as a command to the disciples to serve the outcast. They are to feed the gathered, hungry multitude at their eucharistic feast, and they do this to remember Jesus, to make him present by embodying his ministry, the in-breaking of the Kingdom, in their own lives and ministry.

If we turn to Mark's account of this meal (Mark 6:30–44), moreover, we find it even more instructive for defining the place of Jesus' last supper in relation to his broader meal ministry. In Mark, the disciples have just returned from their mission preaching the gospel to the countryside, and we're told that Jesus calls them away to a quiet place, to reflect on their mission and, presumably, to share fellowship with one another. But a crowd follows them there, disturbing their quiet retreat. As the end of the day nears, the disciples remind Jesus of their desire to share a quiet meal together, and Jesus responds that their first call is to feed those who come to them hungry. And so the crowd is gathered on the grass, and the disciples serve at a eucharist—at a kingdom feast where the multitude are fed—while Jesus presides.

A popular interpretation of Jesus' last supper argues that this meal among intimates stands apart from Jesus' broader practice of table fellowship—that it culminates a series of meals between Jesus and his disciples and that Jesus' command to do this is a command to continue this practice of intimate, exclusive meals. This suggestion has little support in the biblical text. Not only are we offered no set of stories narrating Jesus' practice of sharing table fellowship with his disciples apart from the crowds, but we also find in the one place where the disciples suggest such an exclusive feast, Jesus rebukes them and asks them to be the true elder brother, serving those who have come to them hungry and lost.

When Jesus, therefore, asks his disciples at his last supper with them to break bread and share table fellowship to remember him, he is cluing them in to the essential role that his practice of table fellowship must play in their understanding of his story. Luke has clearly taken this clue. Through it, we see Jesus' story as the story of his gift of himself in table fellowship to those who are alienated from his father—both those who are prodigal and those who have isolated themselves in pious observance—and we have noted that this gift of himself truly cost him his life. We have seen, moreover, that Luke closely ties this gift to Jesus' call to repentance, but that the relationship between gift and repentance is chronologically variable. Repentance could either precede or follow the gift of fellowship. Theologically, however, it is evident that repentance is wholly dependent on the gift, though it is also necessary to some degree for the reception of the gift. Sinners could not dine with Jesus if they were not willing to come to the table; Pharisees who came to the table nonetheless missed out on the gift through their refusal to receive it. But the gift was given—Jesus sat at table with the outcast and the religiously devout—whatever degree of repentance had been offered. We have, finally, been led to consistently name the gift that Jesus gives of himself, the gift of the Kingdom that he preached—that by giving himself at table, the Kingdom was breaking in through a duly constituted Kingdom feast.

The central mission of the Virginia Seminary is to train leaders for the Church. Under Martha Horne's guidance, seminary formation was guided by a scriptural vision of evangelical hospitality that I have explored in this article. Such a hospitality recognizes and affirms the need for changed lives, that our world is broken and in need of repentance. But this hospitality is grounded even more deeply in the recognition that change and healing in our lives comes first from God's grace—God's gift of God's self in Jesus. We turn to God not to receive God's embrace, but because we have already experienced God's embrace and have found it to be life. We become ministers of God's hospitality, then, in our desire to share this life more broadly, even as we live into it more fully through our very act of sharing. We join Jesus as true elder brothers and sisters, yearning for the return of lost siblings who have wandered far from the love of God. As we have found the unwavering embrace of this love in our continual failings, so we wish to share this embrace, as well.

The locus of this evangelical hospitality will always be the concrete communities of disciples that Jesus has called to follow him. My insight into this hospitality has developed through my exploration of God's hospitality with Christian communities who embody it through their practice of the open table. Opening the table is a controversial practice in the Church, and it may not capture fully the whole of the gospel revealed in Jesus. But it has certainly held up to the Church the significance of evangelical hospitality in the ministry of Jesus and, hence, in the ministry of his Church. As such, it bears further exploration by the broader Church, to discern how Christ would lead his Church into a more faithful ministry.

Notes

1   See John Koenig, *New Testament Hospitality: Partnership with Strangers as Promise and Mission*, (Philadelphia: Fortress Press, 1985) 86–91 for a more complete discussion of this.

2   Lee Edward Klosinski, *The Meals in Mark* (Ann Arbor: University Microfilms, 1988), 56–58. See also Peter Farb and George Armelagos, *Consuming Passions: The Anthropology of Eating* (Boston: Houghton Mifflin, 1980) 4, 211. Taken from John Dominic Crossan, *Jesus: A Revolutionary Biography* (New York: HarperCollins Publishers, 1995) 68–69.

3   Gillian Feeley-Harnik, *The Lord's Table: Eucharist and Passover in Early Christianity* (Philadelphia: The University of Pennsylvania Press, 1981), 71–106.

4   Crossan, *Jesus.*

5   See Feeley-Harnik, 71.

6   See Luke Timothy Johnson, *The Gospel of Luke* (Collegeville, MN: The Liturgical Press, 1991), 97.

The Vocation for Unity in Theological Education

Mitzi J. Budde

A s Christians, we have a God-given unity in Christ that is an enduring gift of grace by the power of the Holy Spirit. We cannot earn it; we cannot create it; we cannot undo it even if we deny it. This unity flows under and through all that we are and all that we do in our separate Christian communities: congregations, denominations, seminaries. This unity is grounded in baptism in the name of the Father, Son, and Holy Spirit, nurtured wherever the gospel is preached and the creeds confessed, and fed whenever the eucharistic meal is celebrated. It is a unity across geographic and political borders. It is a unity that praises God across time and space with all Christians who have lived anywhere and anytime in history, as we bear witness in the eucharistic preface: " . . . joining our voices with Angels and Archangels and with all the company of heaven . . ."[1] This is a unity that cannot be broken.

Conversely, there is a level of unity which is broken among Christians in this earthly pilgrimage at this point in history. This is the brokenness that manifests itself in denominational boundaries and inter- and intra-denominational fights. Christians are called to build bridges across these chasms to make a shared witness to Jesus Christ that will be coherent to an unbelieving world. We are called to recognize the body of Christ, the Church, in those who worship differently from us. We are called into dialogue in order to seek to heal the divisions that have broken the essential unity of the Church.[2]

Church leaders need an ecumenical vision to recognize the deep God-given unity that we share and, arising out of that vision, a vocation that seeks to heal the wounds of disunity in the Church and in the world. This ecumenical vision does not deny the historical complexities of Christian division, nor does it seek to ignore them in the present in favor of some cheap or superficial unity. Rather, it brings the gifts of each tradition to the service of the whole Church. It articulates each tradition's historical critique and unique perspective for the good of the whole Church and builds bridges of dialogue and prayer. This primary Christian vocation is needed now more than ever in a society, church, and world riven by discord, disagreement, and division. Ecumenical rapprochement is the work of the Holy Spirit who moves within the Church to allow it to recognize the unity that is already in its midst through Christ's death and resurrection.

What would it look like for seminaries to be places where the vocation of Christian unity is discussed, fostered, taught, and lived? Can denominational seminaries become places that address and interpret their denominationally distinctive theological heritage and perspective in the context of Christian unity? This paper argues that denominational theological education is greatly strengthened when an intentional ecumenical component is integrated into the curriculum, the formation process, and community life, and seeks to describe how seminaries can do so for the preparation of ecumenically literate ordained and lay leaders in the church.

These are somewhat controversial assertions. Many in the Church today would claim that ecumenism was a twentieth-century optimistic attempt at unity that has been superseded by a retrenched denominationalism or by internal denominational strife or by post-denominationalism, or by all three combined. These objections cannot be ignored, but neither can this pessimistic view be the final word. Seeking unity as Christians was commanded by our Lord, and prayer for unity among his followers was part of Jesus' last prayer for his disciples.

Why should seminary communities and denominational leaders care about fostering ecumenical vision and vocation in seminary education? Church leaders in the twenty-first century face a complex web of contexts for ministry, many of them inherently ecumenical. Students of all denominations need to be equipped to serve in a religious world that is, paradoxically, both more interconnected and more fragmented than ever before. The changing context of the Church, the seminaries, the ecumenical movement, and the world demands of clergy and lay leaders a solid foundation for the ecumenical aspects of ministry.

The Changing Church

The congregations that American seminarians will serve in the twenty-first century are no longer homogeneous groups of folk raised in that denominational tradition. The average American local parish is an ecumenical experience within its own four walls. Many congregations now include significant numbers of people on a personal ecumenical journey. Many have changed denominations, for various reasons: a mid-life faith awakening, a tragedy that brings soul-searching, a desire for a change in the routine of faith life, a moral conflict with a denomination's chosen ethical stance, a theological dispute, or simply geographic convenience. The number of ecumenical marriages has increased dramatically, and frequently the marriage partners from another tradition attend worship in their spouse's church, though often they do not ever join.

Some laity lack a strong commitment to a theological tradition and are "church shopping," a phenomenon often decried as a negative example of a consumer society. Church choice may be based on sociological or psychological factors. For other laity, however, theological issues are decisive, but those issues have transcended denominational branding. What may look on the surface to be "church shopping" may actually be a layperson's search for a parish with preaching, liturgy, and hymnody that fit his/her own worldview. The old barriers of family church affiliation, loyalty to a denominational tradition, or interpretation of one's tradition as the only "true" church have, for the most part, broken down in American church society. In spite of the inevitable sense of loss that denominational mobility might represent in American religious life, the positive side of this phenomenon reflects the success of the ecumenical movement. In making these denominational switches, these laity have found a common confession, a faithful sacramental life, a valid ministry, and a shared mission of outreach (the definition of *koinonia* per the 1991 World Council of Churches Canberra Assembly) in another denomination.

How are seminary graduates prepared to deal with this new phenomenon? Successful parish clergy are able to speak to these ecumenical laity intelligently, respectfully, and in theologically articulate ways. Ecumenism at the local level in the twenty-first century is no longer primarily the relationship with the parish down the street (as important as that might continue to be). Rather, the new ecumenism begins within the walls and pews of each congregation. An informed knowledge of other denominations and of the ecumenical movement is now an essential part of effective parish ministry.

The Changing Seminaries

Like the laity within their congregations, many seminarians today are not "cradle" members of their denomination. Many students have extensive experience in another denomination, some in several other denominations. Some students contrast their previous church experience negatively with the denomination that has now captured their hearts and allegiance, which can then lead to an anti-ecumenical spirit. Conversely, those born and raised within the denomination are often innocent of any significant direct experience with other denominations. Seminarians may lack an adequate framework to develop a mature ecumenical articulation without guidance.

Rather than fostering an ecumenical vision within the context of denominational identity, however, seminaries often react to this variety of student backgrounds by seeking to inculcate a strong denominational identity in future clergy and lay leaders. The *Princeton Proposal for Christian Unity* points out that as leaders are educated for a particular denominational context, they are "socialized into the particulars that have divided them."[3] Sometimes that socialization becomes framed as if denominational identity were in competition with ecumenical openness. The underlying assumption often seems to be that since laypeople aren't "brand-loyal" anymore, professional church leaders need to be all the more so.

On the macro level, seminaries also mirror this tension between denominational identity and ecumenical openness. Many denominational seminaries were founded out of a specific denominational tradition reflected in their governance structures. But as theological education has become more localized and seminarians have become less mobile, the student body has become denominationally diversified at many institutions. Many seminaries hire faculty from other denominational traditions as well. Interdenominational tolerance is not the same as having an ecumenical vocation as an institution, nor is having a strong denominational affiliation necessarily anti-ecumenical.

Juggling the sometimes competing claims of denominational integrity and ecumenical diversity in the community requires institutional discernment of mission.

Another new reality for many Protestant seminaries is non-denominationalism, particularly in the form of admissions applications from students who sense a call to ministry, but who claim no denominational affiliation. These prospective students may have no identified locus for testing that discernment or for practicing that ministry when they finish seminary. Seminarians who will serve parishes of mainline denominations will be challenged to interpret the faith to people who consider themselves Christians but who do not necessarily share their vocabulary nor automatically accept their convictions.

The Changing Ecumenical Movement

Theological education will need to be intentional if there is to be a next generation of ecumenists: "Unless the quest for Christian unity and common witness and service is addressed in concerted fashion and in self-consciously defined courses of study, the ecumenical memory, to say nothing of the ecumenical vision of the future, will be lost."[4] The movement needs a new generation of ecumenical practitioners who are deeply knowledgeable about the ecumenical breakthroughs of the past in order to carry ecumenical dialogue forward into the future.

The beginning of the contemporary ecumenical movement is dated variously to the first International Missionary Council in 1910, the organization of the World Council of Churches in 1948, or the Roman Catholic Church's Second Vatican Council in 1964. Any of these dates would indicate that the movement has moved well beyond its initiating generation of ecumenists. Yet the training and preparation of leaders in the ecumenical movement has usually been left to chance. In her essay "On Ecumenical Formation," Peggy Way shared her experience of serving in an ecumenical dialogue for the first time, as a member of the Executive Committee of the Consultation on Church Union (COCU). She described her "formation by experience model" in this way: "I quite literally 'picked it up' as I went along, experiencing its processes, listening to dialogue about the issues, intrigued by its conflicts, somewhat intimidated by its leadership, and exalting in its worship. But I was not intentionally nurtured in its concepts or histories."[5]

Several of the bilateral dialogues have expressed the hope that their ecumenical work would make a difference in theological education. The Lutheran-Roman Catholic Dialogue developed the theme in its 1980 report, *Ways to Community*: "Since both the success and failure of ecumenical rapprochement depend heavily on the church's ministers, stress must be laid on their acquiring *ecumenical awareness and experience.* Ecumenical awareness needs to be developed by permeating *theological education* with ecumenism."[6] The Anglican-Methodist dialogue document of 1996, *Sharing in the Apostolic Communion*, suggested that "joint courses might be offered in theological schools" as a way of drawing the two communions closer to one another.[7] *Called to Common Mission*, the Lutheran-Episcopal full-communion agreement that went into effect on January 6, 2001, included a basic provision that "Each church also promises to encourage its people to study each other's basic documents."[8]

Over the past forty years, there has been much ecumenical progress, both in multilateral and bilateral ecumenism. Yet there is much left to do in ecumenical discussions, both bilateral and multilateral. The first of three World Council of Churches studies on ethics and moral formation, *Costly Unity*, included a plea that "the WCC make an explicit effort to protect and develop such ecumenical memory by consciously creating and sustaining a 'community of elders' in the ecumenical movement . . . The need for adequate ecumenical formation should be honored."[9] The dialogues that are under way at the international, national, regional, and local levels need participants who are informed about what has been achieved in the past in order to build on that foundation for the future.

In the past, ecumenism has been primarily the venue of professional theologians who represented their denomination officially on dialogue teams and spent years reaching formal ecumenical accords. The maturity of the movement means that now clergy and laity in the field can be involved in new ways. Christian Churches Together in the U.S.A., for example, invites new denominations and individuals who do not necessarily represent an entire denomination to the table of ecumenical dialogue. The 2003 *Princeton Proposal for Christian Unity* was developed by theologians and ecumenists who were not official representatives of their churches, and the Proposal calls for the ecumenical involvement of non-specialists in specific ways:

> Church leaders in each place should work to implement existing agreements. In order to promote common mission, lay members should be encouraged to worship and serve in congregations in partner denominations. ... The ecumenical vocation of married couples from separated communions should be acknowledged and supported by the churches. ... God may call lay and ordained members of one church to sustained participation in the life and mission of separated churches, even if sacramental communion is not possible for a time. Such vocations do not deny real theological differences or disrespect canonical order but rather are a call to endure separation as a discipline which sharpens passion for unity. ... The churches should seek to identify and champion these vocations as a gift of the Holy Spirit to the divided churches.[10]

Lutheran pastors, Episcopal priests, and Moravian, Presbyterian, Reformed, and United Church of Christ ministers have opportunities to serve in a clerical exchange with another denomination under the guidelines of recent full-communion agreements.[11] Seminarians will have multiple opportunities to become ecumenists, if they are prepared and educated to be ecumenically informed and committed church leaders.

The Changing World

Ecumenical education is also vital for the Christian witness to a world of many faiths. In a post-September 11, 2001, world, Christians have a new urgency to find unity within Christianity, in order to speak more clearly and to witness more intelligibly in interreligious dialogue. Interreligious dialogue and globalization have become integral parts of theological education today. As J. Paul Rajashekar has written:

> "[A] truly ecumenical theology is engaged in dialogue both internally and externally—internally within the community of faith and externally with those of other faiths and no faith. These dimensions of introspection, critical analysis and open dialogue with the world would not be mutually exclusive but rather interpenetrate and shape our ecumenical self-understanding."[12]

The questions and issues of interfaith relations are pressing in twenty-first-century America. Those questions challenge Christians to respond with an ecumenical voice.

American Christianity is also coming to realize that Christians in other parts of the world, even Christians of their own denomination, have differing theological perspectives, particularly on moral and ethical issues. Several Christian World Communions are in intense conversation and significant division over theological differences. Global perspectives bring new challenges and new urgency to ecumenical and interreligious dialogue.

These ethical dilemmas and discussions are taking place across denominational lines as well as across geographic boundaries. Nearly all American denominations are grappling with ethical discernments such as human sexuality, genetic engineering, end-of-life issues, and just war. Often proponents of one side of a given moral issue find more in common with those of another denomination who share their ethical stance than they find with those on the other side of the ethical divide within their own denominational tradition. The churches can speak with moral authority to society most effectively when they can speak together with common convictions and common principles, even if they cannot speak with unanimity on all difficult issues.

Transmitting an ecumenical spirit to the next generation involves training clergy for ecumenical reception in the local church, developing professional ecumenists who are knowledgeable of past achievements and prepared to continue the work for the future, and inculcating an ecumenical spirit in all church leaders. It takes a clear vision of the unity that we share in Christ despite the fragmentation of the Christian church. It is also the vocation for discipleship: that we all may reflect the unity that Christ shares with the Father (John 17:21).

A Proposal for the Future

Seminaries conscientiously teach students the history of the church's divisions: early church heresies, Reformation disputes, modern denominationalism. Yet we also need to teach the quest for unity. When I teach students, usually I find them well educated about these theological divisions, but *not* about the decades of ecumenical dialogue that have addressed and, in many cases, bridged these divisions. We re-inculcate the divisions of the church into every successive generation.

Transmitting an ecumenical spirit to the next generation will involve training clergy for ecumenical reception in the local church, developing church leaders who are knowledgeable of past ecumenical dialogues and prepared to continue the work for the future, nurturing those who wish to prepare for calls in full-communion partner churches, and inculcating an ecumenical spirit in all church leaders. Adapting the nomenclature of catechesis, I propose a three-part model to a positive ecumenical experience in a denominational seminary context: "inform," "form," and "transform."[13] This paper does not seek to argue that all seminaries ought to have the same approach to ecumenical education and formation, but rather that every seminary should consider carefully its own definition of ecumenical formation and the appropriate integration of ecumenism into the seminary's life and culture. Seminarians need to learn to recognize the marks of the Church (one, holy, apostolic and catholic) in other traditions, as well as to discern the presence (or absence) of those marks in their own. Such discernment is theological, spiritual, and experiential.

Inform

The "inform" dimension begins at the literacy level: teaching the content of ecumenism. One begins by studying the theological constructs of the other church in order to understand it on its own terms before making theological value judgments out of one's own tradition. But this is not a detached intellectual exercise; students can only appropriate this material if it fits into their own theological construal of the Church. Ultimately ecumenics leads to discernment as to whether one finds true church authentically in the other.

The distinction between comparative dogmatics and ecumenical theology is a crucial element to the "inform" stage of ecumenical learning. Seminarians need to acquire at least a basic understanding of other churches' theology, polity, liturgical practices, homiletics, forms of spirituality, and cultures, in a way that engages the other traditions with respect. Clergypersons need enough understanding of other traditions to interpret parishioners' reactions when they respond instinctively out of a different polity. For example, a convert to a tradition that understands its priest or minister as a prophetic leader who stands apart from the congregation might come to a vestry position with an unexamined assumption that the clergyperson is hired staff and a differing expectation about the priest's level of accountability to the governing board of the parish. The same sorts of issues may arise over differences in theology, liturgical practices, etc.

Furthermore, seminarians' understanding of their own tradition is enriched through knowledge of its accomplishments in multilateral and bilateral dialogues and the current issues in the dialogues in which their church is involved. The Roman Catholic Church's *Ecumenical Dimension* document identifies two aspects to teaching the content of ecumenism: 1) a basic course in ecumenism taught as part of the seminary curriculum and 2) permeating other courses in the curriculum (biblical studies, theology, church history, pastoral care, Christian education, etc.) with the results of ecumenical dialogues.[14] Learning to read and assess ecumenical documents, which make up a specialized genre within theological literature, is an important skill.

Once they become congregational leaders, seminary graduates will have the opportunity and the responsibility to bring the ecumenical accords of their own church into the parish's life and practice. As Anglican Stephen Sykes has said: "Ecumenical documents make little or no impact . . . in the short time scale in which we have them. We do not sing them, or pray them, or dance them, or dress them. We study them. That is why they have so little impact."[15] Those agreements will remain merely printed historical documents unless parish leaders are conversant with the dialogue and its results and are open to ecumenical reception at the parish level. Church leaders for the next generation are called to inspire the Church by translating the theological documents of the ecumenical agreements into the living, singing, praying life of the local church. Incorporating an informed dimension into theological education "aims beyond teaching, to the building up of an ecumenically oriented theology: it is in itself a reflection and a contribution to dialogue and research."[16]

Form

The "form" stage of education looks beyond the curriculum to include formal and informal experiences within the seminary community. Groome calls this stage the "affective/relational" dimension, characterized by students' growth as "agent-subjects-*in-relationship*," relationship with God, community and the world.[17] To form seminarians ecumenically means to move beyond the intellectual learnings of the "inform" stage to a level of experiential education characterized by relationship and encounter.

The "implicit curriculum" (the cultural and socialization approaches of the community of learning) and the "null curriculum" (that which is taught by omission) also play significant roles in the "form" stage.[18] At seminaries, the implicit curriculum includes chapel practices, formation groups, spiritual direction, field education, retreats, and informal groups. A seminary with an ecumenically diverse student body offers an environment which can be a rich encounter with other ways of talking about and to God. Ecumenically integrated formation groups give students a chance to share the experiences that they have had with other Christian communities, both positive and negative, to confront their stereotypes about others, and to reflect theologically on those experiences.

Spiritual ecumenism is at the heart of ecumenical encounter. As Walter Kasper notes, ecumenical education is a "catechetical, homiletic, theological endeavour, but even more a spiritual renewal and a new start."[19] Beyond attending other churches' worship services as observers, seminarians are enriched by opportunities to pray and worship with others. Seminaries whose chapel practices include liturgies from other denominational traditions and ecumenical worship experiences are providing an experiential ecumenical component. Prayer for unity creates a hunger for unity.

Future congregational leaders need to be equipped to translate ecumenical agreements into a local church's pastoral practice and spiritual life. Newly ordained ministers will find themselves dealing with ecumenical issues in the parish such as mixed marriages and pastoral issues (i.e. premarital counseling, baptisms, first communion), blended worship opportunities (both community worship events and bilateral worship with neighboring congregations of other denominations), joint education opportunities (such as Vacation Bible School and joint youth groups), and shared service opportunities (like Habitat for Humanity, literacy tutoring, and food pantries).

An example of an implicit curriculum element is the inclusion of faculty not of the dominant denominational tradition in the seminary's student evaluation process for ordination. Such a practice implies recognition of the validity of other churches' ministries and discernment processes regarding ordination. A seminary's openness to faculty of other traditions and a campus environment that values ecumenical diversity is a positive form of implicit curriculum. The high institutional commitments that seminaries demonstrate in their membership in theological consortia are also positive implicit curriculum factors.

The null curriculum is "what the community does not talk about, who is not seen gathering with the community."[20] If courses in ecumenism are not offered, or are offered only infrequently, that lacuna becomes a form of null curriculum. The lack of the presence—or the acknowledgement—of adherents of other denominational traditions in a seminary community is also a null curriculum element. Choosing not to observe the Week of Prayer for Christian Unity or some other form of ecumenical worship experience in seminary chapel practice is another null curriculum example.

Transform

The third phase of the educational experience, one that seeks to transform, moves beyond learning that is outside of oneself to conversion: connecting the subject deeply with students' lives and faith systems. This transformative learning is not only for the individual students, however, but rather includes a component of community transformation as well. For the specific topic of ecumenism, this stage involves fostering an ecumenical spirit in students and in the institution as a whole. Emmanuel Sullivan identifies this aspect as "development of a *sensus fidei oecumenicae*—an instinct for an ecumenical faith."[21] Every aspect of the seminary experience teaches, whether through the explicit curriculum, the implicit curriculum, or the null curriculum. Ultimately, every component speaks about what the institutional community values, believes, and confesses.

Jack Mezirow, the educational theorist who first identified transformative learning as a critical element of adult education, describes this type of learning as having four stages or processes: identifying the content and assumptions of one's beginning life perspective or worldview, developing new possibilities, transforming one's original perspectives to accommodate a new perspective, and becoming a newly integrated self. "The job of adult educators is to help learners look critically at their beliefs and behaviors, not only as these appear at the moment but in the context of their history (purpose) and consequences in the learners' lives."[22] Developing a methodology for fostering experiences of transformative learning, however, can be a challenge. Transformation cannot be scripted.

Transformative learning is a process of change and challenge to one's old worldview that may have painful elements. Yet the challenges of change are integral to all true educational endeavors. The teacher's role as "leading learner," e.g., one open to the educational process and seeking to grow and learn alongside his/her students, is vital.[23] Theological seminaries are enriched by having faculty members who represent multiple traditions, are involved in ecumenical dialogues, and who are conversant across Christian traditions, in order to create a community of learning that reflects the whole church.

Education for Implementing Full-Communion Agreements

The full-communion agreements now in place create a new challenge for denominational theological education within those traditions. At present, the denominations that have full-communion agreements are not yet preparing their students to serve in the other denomination's parishes. Thoroughly preparing students for service in another tradition would impact theology, homiletics, liturgics, spirituality, polity, field education, and the culture of the other church. One beginning would be to develop an overview course focused on a church's full-communion partners, which would cover the differing theologies, polities, liturgies, and spiritual practices of those partner churches. The partner churches' liturgies could be integrated into liturgics courses and chapel worship services. Guest preachers from those traditions could demonstrate the churches' differing emphases in homiletics. Guest speakers could model the tradition in word and presence. Students of partner churches could attend short-term intensive courses at a partner church's campus if exchange programs were created.

To help seminarians explore the different ethos and cultures of partner churches, interested students might be partnered with a mentor from the other tradition for a period of time. A spiritual director from another tradition might be enlightening. Some students might seek a field education placement in a church of another tradition. Incorporating discussion of the denominational theological differences behind pastoral encounters with intentionality into Clinical Pastoral Education might be enlightening for students.

There are differences in practices that must be understood if one hopes to serve in another church effectively. A Lutheran pastor, coming from a tradition with no canon law, will be unable to serve an Episcopal congregation well under the full-communion provisions for clergy interchangeability without some knowledge of Episcopal canon law. An Episcopal priest, conversely, will be quite lost in a Lutheran setting unless he/she understands the ways that the constitutions of the ELCA, the synod, and the congregation cover procedural provisions in a way analogous to Episcopal canon law. How to seek a placement in another church is another area of significant difference. ELCA pastors must apply for congregational placements through the synodical bishop; in many Episcopal dioceses, priests may send a resume directly to the parish. Seminary panel discussions with representatives of several traditions might address special topics of such distinctive denominational practices.

Because it would be impossible to prepare every student for all the potential full-communion exchanges, faculty advisors might encourage students to consider their vocational goals within ministry and to envision which ecumenical options they might wish to study. The faculty might identify certain students with potential gifts for ecumenical service and encourage them to seek preparation through their elective course choices. Asking those clergypersons who have chosen a placement in another tradition to reflect on what preparation they wish that they had had in order to be better equipped for this call would provide useful outcomes assessment.

Thus far, both Lutherans and Episcopalians have continued the policy by which seminarians are allowed to attend a seminary of the other tradition for up to two years but then must spend a minimum of one year in the seminary of their own tradition. At what point ought that requirement to change in a mature full-communion relationship?

Conclusion

Denominational seminary communities themselves need trans-formation. The goal ought to be that described by the Yahara conference, to develop "a vision of an ecumenically renewed and reconstructed theological education, radically transformed in faithfulness to the ongoing search to understand the nature of God and to comprehend God's action in Christ. Theological educators . . . are called to reconceive, re-envision, and redirect the whole enterprise!"[24]

Seminaries can and should be communities that articulate the vision of who we are in Christ, as a church and as individu-als, and what that means for how we relate to other Christians, to those of other faiths, and to those of no faith at all. Instead, we often define ourselves more by distinctives than by com-monalities and pride ourselves on our differences. While we cannot create unity, as Christian communities we can create an environment that values it. We can provide a language and a framework that seeks rapprochement. And we can live together in shared witness to that ultimate reality that is our true unity in Christ.

Ultimately, an ecumenical heart and spirit cannot be in-culcated by another. Openness to others of the family of Jesus Christ who profess a different confession from one's own is a gift through the power of the Holy Spirit. Nonetheless, a seminary culture infused with ecumenical appreciation and awareness is fertile soil for the planting and nurturing of an ecumenical spirit in students, with prayer that God will give the growth by grace.

Notes

1   The Episcopal Church, *The Book of Common Prayer* (New York: Church Hymnal Corp., 1979), 362.

2   I am indebted to Michael Root for articulating the two types of unity in his essay "Essential Unity and Lived Communion: The Interrelation of the Unity We Have and the Unity We Seek" in *The Ecumenical Future: Background Papers for In One Body Through The Cross,* Carl E. Braaten and Robert W. Jenson, eds. (Grand Rapids: Eerdmans, 2004), 106–25.

3   Carl E. Braaten and Robert W. Jenson, eds. *In One Body through the Cross: The Princeton Proposal for Christian Unity* (Grand Rapids: Eerdmans, 2003), 54.

4   Daniel Martensen, "Introduction," in *The Teaching of Ecumenics*, Samuel Amirtham and Cyris H.S. Moon, eds. (Geneva: WCC Publications, 1987), xii.

5   Peggy Way, "On Ecumenical Formation," in *The Vision of Christian Unity*, Thomas F. Best and Theodore J. Nottingham, eds. (Indianapolis: Oikoumene Publications, 1997), 206.

6   Michael Kinnamon and Brian E. Cope, eds., *The Ecumenical Movement: An Anthology of Key Texts and Voices* (Geneva: WCC Publications, 1997), 230.

7   Anglican-Methodist Dialogue, "Sharing in the Apostolic Communion," in *Growth in Agreement II*, Jeffrey Gros, Harding Meyer, and William G. Rusch, eds. (Geneva: WCC Publications, 2000), 59.

8   Episcopal Church and Evangelical Lutheran Church in America, *Called to Common Mission*, http://archive.elca.org/ecumenical/ fullCommunion/Episcopal/ccmresources/index.html, 4.

9   "Costly Unity" in *Ecclesiology and Ethics*, Thomas F. Best and Martin Robra, eds. (Geneva: WCC Publications, 1997), 21.

10 Braaten and Jenson, *In One Body Through the Cross*, 55.

11 See Episcopal Church and Evangelical Lutheran Church in America, *The Orderly Exchange of Pastors and Priests Under Called to Common Mission*, http://www.episcopalchurch.org/1521_29251_ ENG_HTM.htm; and Evangelical Lutheran Church in America, Presbyterian Church (U.S.A.), Reformed Church in America, United Church of Christ, *The Orderly Exchange of Ordained Ministers of Word and Sacrament*, http://archive.elca.org/ministry/ pdf/formula.pdf; Evangelical Lutheran Church in America, Moravian Church in America, *Principles for the Orderly Exchange of Ordained Ministers of Word and Sacrament*, http://archive.elca. org/ecumenical/FullCommunion/Moravian/orderlyexchange/ index.html.

12 J. Paul Rajashekar, "Dialogue with People of Other Faiths and Ecumenical Theology," in *The Teaching of Ecumenics, 84.*

13 See Thomas H. Groome, *Sharing Faith* (San Francisco: HarperSanFrancisco, 1991), 18–21, and Jane Regan, *Toward an Adult Church: A Vision of Faith Formation* (Chicago: Loyola Press, 2003), 15–17.

14 Pontifical Council for Promoting Christian Unity, *The Ecumenical Dimension in the Formation of Those Engaged in Pastoral Work* (Vatican City: Vatican, 1997), 4.

15 Stephen Sykes, "Lutheranism and the Ecumenical Movement: An Anglican Perspective," *LWF Documentation 32* (March 1993): 40.

16 Jos E. Vercruysse, "Questionnaire on the Teaching of Ecumenics: An Evaluation of the Responses," *Centro Pro Unione Bulletin* 46 (Fall 1994): 22.

17 Groome, 20.

18 Elliot W. Eisner, *The Educational Imagination*, third ed. (Upper Saddle River, NJ: Prentice Hall, 1994), 87, 97.

19 Walter Kasper, "The Present Situation and Future of the Ecumenical Movement," November 17, 2001, http://www.vatican. va/roman_curia/pontifical_councils/chrstuni/documents/rc_pc_ chrstuni_doc_20011117_kasper-prolusio_en.html, 5.

20 Regan, 16.

21 Sullivan, "Reception of Ecumenism," in *Twelve Tales Untold*, John T. Ford and Darlis J. Swan, eds. (Grand Rapids: Eerdmans, 1993), 142.

22 Jack Mezirow, *Transformative Dimension of Adult Learning* (San Francisco: Jossey-Bass, 1991), 197–98, 212.

23 Groome, 449–50.

24 Russell E. Richey, ed., *Ecumenical & Interreligious Perspectives: Globalization in Theological Education* (Nashville: The United Methodist Board of Higher Education and Ministry, 1992), 127.

Outside the Camp: *Imitatio Christi* and Social Ethics in Hebrews 13:10–14

A. Katherine Grieb

Introduction

The Epistle to the Hebrews is consistently overlooked as a resource for Christian social ethics, even though its author calls it a "word of exhortation" (13:22),[1] its highly sophisticated rhetoric binds christological meditation and ethical exhortation throughout the address,[2] and its final chapter deals almost exclusively with material that, anywhere else in Holy Scripture, would be self-evidently relevant to the formation and nurture of Christian communities and so a matter of ethics. It stresses the love of the brothers and sisters, hospitality to strangers, solidarity with the suffering, the sanctity of marriage, money and possessions, the sharing of resources, and support of leaders.

When the ethics of Hebrews 13 are noted, they are often not appreciated. Knut Backhaus begins his article on ethics in Hebrews 13 by listing the charges brought against this section by other commentators.[3] Some charge that Hebrews 13 is "self-referential and trivial," disproportionate to its masterful theology; others charge that the ethics are "separationist and esoteric," that the group claims are disproportionate to the universal tendencies of the theology of chapters 1–12. If the point of Hebrews is taken to be the exposition of the Son's high priesthood, the argument structured in a great chiasm from 5:11 to 10:32, then Hebrews 13 looks like a useless appendix; whereas if the argument is conceived in a more linear way, reaching its rhetorical climax in the great exposition of faith in chapter 11 and its aftermath, the ethical injunctions seem unimpressive, as if the theological elephant had labored to bring forth at last a moral mouse![4]

Hebrews may be suffering from its close association with the Pauline epistles and the still widely held view that the structure of Paul's letters must conform to the indicative/imperative structure of his thought. The model for this is Romans, where after doing eleven chapters of theology, Paul is thought to begin doing ethics with the great "therefore" of 12:1. This "first theological exposition, then moral exhortation" model is then extrapolated to the rest of Paul's letters and so also to Hebrews. The problem, as Wayne Meeks has argued,[5] is that it doesn't even really work for Romans, let alone the rest of Paul's letters. It certainly doesn't work for Hebrews: a quick glance at the relationship between christological argument and ethical injunction will show that they are carefully interwoven throughout the sermon.[6]

In this brief essay, I will focus on a passage in Hebrews 13 where christology and ethics are integrated in a remarkable way: the five verses of 13:10–14 where the death of Christ as a criminal on the cross is provocatively reconceptualized as "an altar" (sacrifice) in which members of the community partake. Their participation in him is tied to their imitation of him: just as he suffered "outside the gate," like the sacrificial animals who were killed and whose bodies were burned "outside the camp" on Yom Kippur, so the community is to go to him, "outside the camp," identifying not with the privileged and the powerful, but with those who resemble their Lord as he died.

The use of *imitatio Christi* as a warrant for social ethics is hardly unique to Hebrews: it appears prominently in Paul, the Fourth Gospel, the synoptics, James, and Revelation. What is distinctive about the ethics of Hebrews is its use of *imitatio Christi* to warrant solidarity with those who are politically at risk and suffering hardship. Even stronger than the "do unto the least of these" ethics of Matthew 25 is the "become identi-fied with" ethics of Hebrews 13. And this is precisely the per-fect conclusion for an argument that has stressed the radical identification of the Son himself with humanity as a necessary component of his perfection as our great high priest. The com-munity that now identifies with him imitates not his sinlessness or his saving death on our behalf, the once-for-all sacrifice to end all sacrifices of that kind, but it does imitate the two-fold movement of the Son's "going in" and his "going out"—in the community's own entrance into the sanctuary to approach the heavenly throne and in its exodus toward a place it does not yet know as it waits for the promised city to come.

I will argue that the examples of Abraham (and Sarah) in 11:8–16, who are leaving what they know to seek a city that is *about* to be, and the example of Moses in 11:24–26, who "considered abuse suffered for the Christ to be greater wealth than the treasures of Egypt" and therefore joined the cause of the Israelites against Pharaoh, anticipate the exhortation to the community of Jesus Christ in 13:13 to join in solidarity with him in an errand of mercy. The argument of 13:10–14 forms a triptych: it is framed in a tight triplicate structure of sacrifice and solidarity: just as the bodies of the animals whose blood is a sacrifice for sin are burned "outside the camp" (13:11), so

Jesus "also suffered outside the city gate in order to sanctify the people by his own blood" (13:12). So "let us then go to him outside the camp and bear the abuse he endured" (13:13). Since, in the context of the larger argument of Hebrews, "going to him" may also serve as an exhortation to martyrdom if necessary, a glance at Origen will also be useful.

The Structure of the Argument

Hebrews 13:10–14 is surrounded by ethical injunctions on either side, mostly in the imperative mood. Prior to our passage, the author requires both *philadelphia* and *philoxenia*, love of brothers and sisters and hospitality to strangers. The love for insiders apparently needs no warrant, but the injunction to welcome strangers is supported by the reminder that they may be angels traveling *incognito*, as were the three visitors to Abraham and Sarah in Genesis 18. Hebrews 13:3 ("remember those in prison, as though in fetters with them and those being treated badly as if you were in their bodies"[7]) directly anticipates our passage. Marriage and the marriage bed are defiled at the risk of God's judgment on sexual immorality and adultery. The author advocates a life preferring contentment to love of money. The warrant given for that recommendation is God's promise in Deuteronomy 31:6 and 8 (also Joshua 1:5) "I will never leave you or forsake you" (translation mine). But the next verse assumes a more sinister tone as the author prompts the community to say the words of Psalm 118:6, "The Lord is my helper; I will not be afraid. What can anyone do to me?" More than the possible deprivation of money is clearly at stake here.

The meaning of 13:7 is disputed: as the community remembers their leaders, especially those who spoke the word of God to them, they are to consider the outcome of their lives and to imitate their faith or faithfulness. Does this imply that some or most of those leaders have faced martyrdom? Certainly the great list, too many to name, of heroes faithful unto death of chapter 11 is somehow being referenced as the community's leaders are commended. The pronouncement in the indicative ("Jesus Christ is the same, yesterday, today, and forever") could possibly refer back to those other largely unsurprising imperatives. As Matera suggests, the problem Hebrews deals with is not that the addressees do not know what they should do, but that they do not do what they should know.[8] On the other hand, 13:8 could also serve as a contrast to 13:9 so that the solid sameness of Jesus Christ is to be preferred to the diverse and strange teachings that are compared to foods that do not benefit the ones "walking" that way. The author has mixed his metaphors, perhaps to pick up the idea of *halakah* (walking in the way of righteousness), but we get his point: just as there is junk food, so there is junk christology. Rhetorically, the contrast sets up its opposite: solid christology, the way of the cross, the way of "outside the camp."[9]

The typological structure of the argument is clear: I have already noted the *inclusio* of *echomen* that begins 13:10 and 13:14. Notice also how tightly constructed the passage is in terms of its logical connectives: *gar, dio, toinun,* and another *gar* show the precise way that the statements follow upon one another. Hebrews 13:11 functions as the warrant for the statement that "we have an altar" by supplying not just the historical memory (in Hebrews, the word of God is living and active, cf. 4:12–13) but also the way God has set things up typologically, as shown by that word. The force of the *dio* in 13:12 is to show the corresponding antitype in Christ: it is a theological necessity for the two stories to match, since Jesus Christ *is* God's living and active word. And it is an ethical necessity in 13:13 for the story of the community to provide the corresponding type in the present situation. The final *gar* in 13:14 provides another warrant: the eschatological framework that relativizes all human politics (*polis*) in the light of God's reality, God's promise of the city that is still to come.

The reference to the "abiding city" which we do not have in

13:14 refers back to the "city" sought by Abraham and Sarah, "the city that has foundations, whose builder and maker is God" (11:10), the city that God has prepared (13:16) for all those who see themselves as strangers and exiles on earth. As our author points out, "people who talk like that" about themselves (who are not ashamed to be identified with the disenfranchised and powerless) are precisely those of whom God is not ashamed to be called their God (11:16).[10] There are other references back to Hebrews 11. "Seeking" the city in 13:14 echoes the language of those seeking a fatherland in 11:14; the description of the city as "about to be" (coming into existence) matches the language in 11:8 describing the unknown place that Abraham was "about to receive" as an inheritance. For all Abraham knows, he could have been handed the deed to "oceanfront property in Arizona."[11]

In addition to the Abraham links, there is a prominent Moses connection in 13:13 where the community is instructed to "bear the abuse" that Christ endured. Their model is Moses in 11:24–26, who grew up in the splendor of Pharaoh's palace but "refused to be called the son of Pharaoh's daughter" (his claim to high status and privilege), "choosing to share ill-treatment with the people of God instead of enjoying the fleeting pleasures of sin." The community has already been enjoined in 13:3 to remember those who are "ill-treated" (prisoners who are being tortured or others who are suffering at the hands of the powers and principalities) as if they themselves were inhabiting the bodies of those so misused. The author glosses Moses' decision not only as an ethical choice but also as a theological judgment about reality and illusion: Moses "considered abuse suffered for the Christ to be greater wealth than the treasures of Egypt." The word translated "abuse" (*oneidismon*) appears in both passages.

The most striking structural feature of the passage, of course, is the dramatic threefold repetition of the preposition *exō* in 13:11, 13:12, and 13:13, all the more compelling in an argument that has focused so much on "approaching" and "entering."[12] Wedderburn, arguing for separate authorship for chapter 13, frames the question provocatively: "Are we then to assume that, for the author of chapter 13 at least, the thoroughly profane world 'outside the camp' has, in a most daring paradox, now become the equivalent of the 'holy of holies,' the most holy inner sanctuary?"[13] Wedderburn seems to intend this question as a *reductio ad absurdum*, but, as someone who thinks the same theologian wrote chapters 1–12 and chapter 13, I would answer his question affirmatively: in a most daring paradox, our author has identified the crucifixion of Jesus of Nazareth on a pagan Roman cross surrounded by skulls near the city dump, about as unclean as you can get, with the solemn entrance of the holiest man in Israel on the holiest day of the year into the holiest place in the world.

The *eisodos* into the sacred space of the sanctuary is accomplished first by Jesus, as the forerunner and path maker, but the community is urged to have confidence to enter through his blood (10:19–20); in the same way, the community is reminded of his *exodos* and its own identity as "holy partners in a heavenly calling" just at the point where Jesus is called "the apostle" (uniquely in the New Testament) as well as the high priest of our confession (3:1–2), and where his faithfulness (his faithful obedient self-offering on the cross) is also mentioned. Hebrews 11 makes it clear that the *exodos* in view is a departure from the status of the privileged and the powerful as well as from the geography of the dominant culture of deadly Egypt.

Together, these three locations "outside" form a literary triptych like the triptych of an ancient altarpiece.[14] The suffering of Jesus Christ "outside the city gate" comprises the larger center panel; the two wing panels "outside the camp" show, on the one side, the dead sacrificial animals (paradoxically described as *zōōn* as in Romans 12:1) and, on the other side, the Christian community (paradoxically alive, sanctified, rescued from death by the blood of Jesus) identified with those in danger of being sacrificed to death. If this is correct, then Hebrews 13:14 functions liturgically as the *missa est* whereby the community is enjoined not, I think, to abandon false ritual or religion (ritual is valued positively in Hebrews, as it is in the Apocalypse), but to leave the altar *in imitatio Christi* in service to those in need. The literary structure of the passage implies a verbal ikon, a triptych whose construction is classically typological: figures and events from Israel's history (Abraham and Sarah, Moses, and the bodies of those dead "living beings" outside the camp described, e.g., in Leviticus 16:27) anticipate the person and work of Jesus Christ. In the parallel and opposite construction, the Christian community is exhorted to imitate the person and work of Jesus Christ by going "outside the camp" to him in the form of assisting those in danger.

Much of my argument depends on reading 13:10 *not* as distancing the community from the levitical priesthood (and certainly not from Judaism itself as it has sometimes been read!),[15] but *instead* as rhetorical heightening of the tremendous privilege of participating in the cross of Christ, the "altar" from which *even* those who serve the tabernacle ("tent" *skēnē*) have no authority to eat. The biblical warrant for the levitical priesthood to partake of certain sacrifices is found at Leviticus 6:16 and 7:6. The community of Christ has the even greater privilege of partaking in his suffering and death, an idea already anticipated in Hebrews 3:14, "For we have become partners of the Christ, if only we hold our first confidence firm to the end."

The rhetorical heightening is necessary because of the terror of the cross and also because of its shame. This is an event that occurs "outside the city gate," outside of respectable society. As Plautus commented, as a convict you must "trudge out beyond the gate . . . arms outspread, with your gibbet on your shoulders."[16] Crucifixions, whether along the Roman roads or just outside the city gate, were public events, designed to deter opposition to Rome in a particularly dramatic way.[17] Jesus, the author tells us in 12:2, endured the cross, despising its shame, and is now seated at the right hand of God in glory. Now, with that great cloud of witnesses from chapter 11 cheering them on, the Christian community is to run its own race. A shameful death might be faced with impunity by a group of brave and committed believers, but martyrs rarely die in community: part of the terror of the cross is its loneliness. Our preacher anticipates what must be the incredible isolation of someone facing martyrdom and inoculates the community against it by providing them with vivid imagery that can be carried into the prison cell and into the arena.

Origen understood this need for vivid re-description of horror, and, as Rowan Greer has commented, "It is impossible to exaggerate the care with which Origen notes details in Scripture."[18] Most of Origen's biblical commentaries were destroyed (not by those who martyred him but by the church), including his commentary on Hebrews.[19] Writing on Leviticus, Origen comments on the phrase "outside the camp" in a section on the high priesthood of Christ as follows:

> And this is what it is to have suffered "outside the camp": outside the heavenly camp of the angels of God which Jacob saw . . . and at the sight of which Jacob said: "This is the camp of God" (Gen 32:2). Hence every earthly place in which we live and in which Christ suffered in the flesh is outside that heavenly camp.[20]

Origen is employing the interpretive device of *gezera shewa* (catchword linkage): since the LXX uses the phrase *parembolē theou autē* at Genesis 32:2, Origen can use it (by way of Hebrews 13:13) to argue that the whole world into which Christ came is "outside the camp."

It is clear that Origen understood the "altar" we have in 13:10 to refer to the sacrificial death of Christ from his comments on Leviticus 1:5.[21] He notes that Leviticus 1:3 had already specified that "he should offer it at the door of the tent of meeting" but then two verses later it says "at the altar which is at the door of the tent of meeting." Origen wonders about the repetition with its increased specificity and concludes, "Perhaps he wanted it understood that the blood of Jesus is shed not only in Jerusalem, where there was the altar and the base of the altar and the tent of meeting, but that this very same blood is also sprinkled on that altar above which is in heaven. . . ." Leviticus 1:5 shows that "Jesus was offered in sacrifice not only for what is on earth but also for what is in heaven." Origen goes on to comment on the two curtains in Hebrews 9:24 and 10:20 and concludes, "If then these are understood to be two curtains through which Jesus as high priest has entered, the sacrifice also must consequently be understood as double, through which he saved what is on earth and what is in heaven."[22]

Still commenting on Leviticus, Origen goes on to remind his hearers, "You have, therefore, the priesthood because you are a 'priestly race' (1 Peter 2:9) and thus you must offer to God 'a sacrifice of praise'" which Origen goes on to gloss as "a sacrifice of prayer, a sacrifice of mercy, a sacrifice of modesty, a sacrifice of justice, and a sacrifice of holiness."[23]

In "An Exhortation to Martyrdom"[24] he adds:

> (V.) "Of old it was said by God to Abraham, 'Come out of your land' (Gen. 12:1). But to us in a short while it will perhaps be said, 'Come out from the whole earth.' It is good to obey him, so that he may presently show us the heavens in which exists what is called the kingdom of heaven."[25]

> (XXX.) "For just as those who served the altar according to the Law of Moses thought they were ministering forgiveness of sins to the people by the blood of goats and bulls (Heb 9:13, 10:4; Ps 50:13), so also the souls of those who have been beheaded for their witness to Jesus (Rev 20:4, 6:9) do not serve the heavenly altar in vain and minister forgiveness of sins to those who pray. At the same time we also know that just as the high priest Jesus the Christ offered himself as a sacrifice (Heb 5:1, 7:27, 8:3, 10:12), so also the priests of whom he is high priest offer themselves as a sacrifice. This is why they are seen near the altar as near their own place."[26]

(XLIV.) Origen cites Heb 10:32–36 and comments, "Therefore, let us, as well, now endure a hard struggle with sufferings, being publicly exposed to abuse and affliction and joyfully accepting the plundering of our property. For we are persuaded we have a better possession that is not earthly or corporeal, but one that is invisible and incorporeal."[27]

Conclusion

These few verses of the final chapter of Hebrews have particular relevance for denominations such as my own Anglican Communion that are torn apart by North/South global economic issues, sexual ethics, and the very real threat of imprisonment and martyrdom in the very parts of the Church that are most at risk economically and also struggling with HIV/AIDS. How will "first world" Christians respond to these crises? If we hear the "word of exhortation" addressed to us in Hebrews, we will respond like Moses.

Rowan Williams comments on this passage, "We are very concerned about whose company we are seen in," but Jesus says, "Whoever wants to be my disciple must take up a cross." Carrying a cross means walking on the way to execution and receiving contempt, scorn and violence from the crowd. When Jesus says, "Pick up your cross" he's saying, "I will see you in my company, in those going out of the camp, to bear his shame and abuse." Where is Jesus? Where can we find him? In those already outside the camp: those on the way to death, in prison, on death row, but also those dying anywhere, the homeless, migrant workers, the mentally disturbed—the ones we instinctively avoid—we are to come to him there. For us to go there is to say to the world that Jesus has not forgotten them.

Williams continues, "Besides, we need to place ourselves where God can see us in the company of Jesus. Seen in Jesus,

God looks at us with compassionate myopia because Jesus says 'These are my friends.' In prayer, God says to us, 'Stand where I can see you' and we say back to God, 'Here I am in the company of Jesus.' If we're ashamed to be seen in his company, then he just might have a problem being seen with us. And yet, he has taken us to himself—carved us on the palms of his hands—and there we are whether we like it or not. Thank God for it."[28]

Just as the levitical high priest entered the sanctuary of the tabernacle through the blood of the atoning victims while their bodies were burnt outside the camp, so Jesus Christ our great high priest has entered into the heavenly sanctuary through his own saving and sanctifying blood at the same time his body was destroyed outside the city of Jerusalem. Now we Christians, as partakers of his altar (placed in an even more privileged position than the levitical high priest) and as those who have through his blood been granted access to the throne of grace, should be in solidarity with those being tortured and otherwise abused as if we were in their bodies (13:3). As "insiders" *through* him, we will appropriately find ourselves outside the camp *with* him (and also with Abraham and Sarah, Moses, and countless others) bearing his abuse on our way to the city that is still to come.

Notes

1 This assumes the integrity of Hebrews 13, *pace* A. J. M. Wedderburn, "The 'Letter' to the Hebrews and Its Thirteenth Chapter," New Test. Stud. 50 (2004) 390–405. For the majority view, see among others H. W. Attridge, *The Epistle to the Hebrews*, Hermeneia Series (Philadelphia: Fortress, 1989), 384 and C. R. Koester, *Hebrews*, AB 36 (New York: Doubleday, 2001), 19–27.

2 Frank J. Matera, "Moral Exhortation: The Relation between Moral Exhortation and Doctrinal Exposition in the Letter to the Hebrews," *Toronto Journal of Theology* 10:2 (1994) 169–82.

3 Knut Backhaus, "How to Entertain Angels: Ethics in the Epistle to the Hebrews," in *Hebrews: Contemporary Methods—New Insights*, ed. Gabriella Gelardini (Leiden: Brill, 2005), 149–75.

4 Backhaus's delightful metaphor prefers mountain and mouse, 149.

5 Wayne A. Meeks, "Judgment and the Brother: Romans 14:1–15:13," in *Tradition and Interpretation in the New Testament*, ed. Gerald F. Hawthorne and Otto Betz. (Grand Rapids: Eerdmans, 1987), 290–300 at 290.

6 See, for example, Matera's summary from the article listed above: exposition 1:5–14, exhortation 2:1–4, exposition 2:5–18; exposition 3:1–6, exhortation 3:7–4:11, transition 4:12–13, exhortation 4:14–16, exposition 5:1–10; exhortation 5:11–6:20, exposition 7:1–10:18, exhortation 10:19–25; exhortation 10:26–39, exposition 11:1–40, exhortation 12:1–13; exhortation 12:14–29, community matters 13:1–17. I part from Matera at his conclusion: "community matters" hardly does justice to the contents of 13:1–17.

7 Translations of Bible passages are mine.

8 Matera, 170–71. This phrasing by Backhaus, 158. See also Thomas L. Schmidt, "Moral Lethargy and the Epistle to the Hebrews," WTJ 54 (1992) 167–73.

9 I would begin a new paragraph at this point, running from 13:10 through 13:14 to highlight the *inclusio* of *echomen* in those two verses. Alternatively, one could end the paragraph to 13:16 to pick up the other sacrifice references. For the purposes of this brief essay, our focus is on 13:10–14.

10 See Mark 8:38, Matthew 10:32–33, Luke 12:8–9. See also G. W. Grogan, "The Old Testament Concept of Solidarity in Hebrews," *Tyndale Bulletin* 49 (1998) 159–73 at 169 for discussion of solidarity with "outsiders."

11 Scholars outside the United States may not recognize this allusion to country/western singer George Strait's lyrics. Arizona is landlocked.

12 Note the compounds *proserchesthai* (4:16, 10:22, 11:6, cf. 7:19, 25) and *eiserchesthai* (4:1, 3, 11; cf. 6:20, 10:19). Attridge comments that the call to enter into God's rest (4:11) and to approach the throne of grace (4:16) or God (7:25) or Mount Zion (12:22) is now exchanged for the call to "go out" (398).

13 Wedderburn, 403.

14 The term *triptychos* ("having three folds") described an ancient Roman writing tablet with three waxed leaves hinged together, and came to refer to anything composed or presented in three parts or sections. I use it in its liturgical sense (an altarpiece or carving in three panels side by side) to suggest its literary function (typological). In classic Christian typology, figures or events in Israel's past (types) anticipate the person and work of Jesus Christ (antitype), while figures and events in the subsequent life of the Church imitate him.

15 Wedderburn comments on 13:10: "Hitherto it was assumed that Christ's sacrifice and priestly service surpassed and superseded the cult of the old covenant, and achieved what that cult sought to effect but could not. Now however, the old and new cults are contrasted with one another in much the same way as Paul stresses the incompatibility between participation in Christian cultic meals and the pagan ones of demons." Wedderburn, 402. There he also translates a quotation from K. Erlemann's "Alt und neu bei Paulus und im Hebräerbrief," TZ 54 (1998) 345–67 at 365: "Torah-observant Jews or Jewish Christians have no part in this altar."

16 Plautus, *Braggart Warrior* 2.4.6–7 (359–60 of the edition cited in Koester, 570).

17 Martin Hengel, *Crucifixion in the Ancient World and the Folly of the Message of the Cross* (London: SCM Press, 1977). Trans. of *Mors turpissima crucis: Die Kreuzigung in der antiken Welt und die 'Torheit' des 'Wortes vom Kreuz'* published in *Rechtfertigung. Festschrift für Ernst Käsemann zum 70 Geburtstag* (Mohr/Siebeck: Tübingen, 1976) with substantial later additions by the author.

18 "Introduction" to Origen, *Classics of Western Spirituality* (Mahwah, NJ: Paulist, 1979), 31.

19 John Anthony McGuckin, ed., *The Westminster Handbook to Origen* (Louisville, KY: Westminster John Knox, 2004), 32.

20 Hans Urs von Balthasar, ed., *Origen: Spirit and Fire: A Thematic Anthology of His Writings*, trans. Robert J. Daly, S.J. (Washington, DC: CUA Press, 1938. ET 1984), 289.

21 John Calvin sees Jesus Christ as "the altar" of Hebrews 13:10 upon which we lay our gifts, cf. *Institutes* 4.18.17: "He is our Pontiff, who has entered the heavenly sanctuary [Heb 9:24] and opens a way for us to enter [Heb 10:20]. He is the altar [Heb 13:10] upon which we lay out gifts, that whatever we venture to do, we may undertake in him." (McNeill/Battles, 1445).

22 *Origen: Spirit and Fire*, 289–90.

23 Ibid., 293.

24 Origen, "An Exhortation to Martyrdom" in *The Classics of Western Spirituality*, Rowan Greer, trans. and ed. (Mahwah, NJ: Paulist, 1979).

25 "An Exhortation to Martyrdom," 43.

26 "An Exhortation to Martyrdom," 62.

27 "An Exhortation to Martyrdom," 74.

28 Archbishop of Canterbury Rowan Williams, from notes taken by the author at Georgetown University, March 30, 2006.

Theological Exegesis
of Genesis 22:
A Case Study in Wrestling
with a Disturbing Scripture

Stephen L. Cook

T he haunting affront of Genesis 22, the *Akedah* ("Binding") or "Near Sacrifice of Isaac," will surely never cease to challenge the community of faith. At the most recent 2008 meetings of the Society of Biblical Literature, held in Boston, a packed audience of hundreds listened as John J. Collins of Yale University again used this text as an example of an ethically and theologically irredeemable passage within the Bible. It was a session on the "Theological Hermeneutics of Christian Scripture," chaired by Beverly Roberts Gaventa of Princeton Theological Seminary, and featuring R.W.L. Moberly of Durham University and Markus Bockmuehl of Keble College, Oxford University, along with Collins.

All three scholars were cautious about recent efforts at theological interpretation, but Collins was especially negative about theological interpretation of scripture that appeared to lack critical distance from ethically suspect biblical texts. There are sections of scripture, Collins insisted, such as Genesis 22 and the conquest accounts of Joshua, that are simply not worth our sustained attention. Attempts at interpretation and appropriation of such passages are exercises at once both wasteful and distasteful. Professor Moberly's time would be better spent elsewhere than on engaging the *Akedah*.

Walter Moberly countered that abandoning a text such as the *Akedah* is theologically premature and surely blind to its depth of meaning. It is doubtful that what Collins objects to about Genesis 22 is the text's real subject matter. A rich variety of interpretation within both Judaism and Christianity has focused on Genesis 22, and none of it has ever seemed to have thought that the text supports child sacrifice. The role of this text within the history of reception has been neither to condone a primitive rite nor to paint a picture of a cruel and immoral God.

Moberly is surely on to something crucial in making this observation. Jews and Christians have never been tempted to murder their children based on their studies of Genesis 22, and, in fact, have found themselves not merely putting up with this challenging text but also acknowledging its centrality to faith and profound spiritual implications. Thus, one finds images of the *Akedah* occupying pride of place at the earliest excavated Jewish synagogues at Beit Alpha and Dura Europus. One finds it as a highlight of Chartres Cathedral, of Ghiberti's panels on the baptistery of Florence, and of Rembrandt's etchings and paintings. One could, in fact, teach an entire course on the many representations of Genesis 22 in art through the ages.

Encouraged by Moberly's brief defense of Genesis 22 at the Boston SBL, let us return to reconsider the theological meaning of this disturbing text, beginning with a renewed close reading of its narrative.

¹After these things God tested Abraham. He said to him, "Abraham!" And he said, "Here I am." ²He said, "Take your son, your only son Isaac, whom you love, and go to the land of Moriah, and offer him there as a burnt offering on one of the mountains that I shall show you." So Abraham rose early in the morning, saddled his donkey, and took two of his young men with him, and his son Isaac; he cut the wood for the burnt offering, and set out and went to the place in the distance that God had shown him. ⁴On the third day Abraham looked up and saw the place far away. ⁵Then Abraham said to his young men, "Stay here with the donkey; the boy and I will go over there; we will worship, and then we will come back to you." ⁶Abraham took the wood of the burnt offering and laid it on his son Isaac, and he himself carried the fire and the knife. So the two of them walked on together. ⁷Isaac said to his father Abraham, "Father!" And he said, "Here I am, my son." He said, "The fire and the wood are here, but where is the lamb for a burnt offering?" ⁸Abraham said, "God himself will provide the lamb for a burnt offering, my son." So the two of them walked on together. ⁹When they came to the place that God had shown him, Abraham built an altar there and laid the wood in order. He bound his son Isaac, and laid him on the altar, on top of the wood. ¹⁰Then Abraham reached out his hand and took the knife to kill his son. ¹¹But the angel of the LORD called to him from heaven, and said, "Abraham, Abraham!" And he said, "Here I am." ¹²He said, "Do not lay your hand on the boy or do anything to him; for now I know that you fear God, since you have not withheld your son, your only son, from me." ¹³And Abraham looked up and saw a ram, caught in a thicket by its horns. Abraham went and took the ram and offered it up as a burnt offering instead of his son. ¹⁴So Abraham called that place "The LORD will provide"; as it is said to this day, "On the mount of the LORD it shall be provided." ¹⁵The angel of the LORD called to Abraham a second time from heaven, ¹⁶and said,

"By myself I have sworn, says the LORD: Because
you have done this, and have not withheld your
son, your only son, [17]I will indeed bless you, and I
will make your offspring as numerous as the stars
of heaven and as the sand that is on the seashore.
And your offspring shall possess the gate of their
enemies, [18]and by your offspring shall all the nations
of the earth gain blessing for themselves, because
you have obeyed my voice." [19]So Abraham returned
to his young men, and they arose and went together
to Beer-sheba; and Abraham lived at Beer-sheba.
(Genesis 22)

I very much doubt we shall ever fully grasp the meaning of
the horrific events of Genesis 22. God's horrible command and
Abraham's willingness to sacrifice his son, Isaac, stretch our efforts at comprehension almost to the breaking point. We strain
to accept the mystery of the episode, just as we do in the case
of that greater, more momentous sacrifice of a beloved son in
scripture. God's awful abandonment of Jesus, God's only begot-
ten son, to Calvary's cross is downright impossible to wrap our
heads around. But there is no evading the facts. The narrator
makes clear in v. 1 that Abraham was definitely not mistaken
about God's terrible command, just as Jesus, two thousand
years later, would not be mistaken in understanding that it was
God's harsh, predetermined will that he also must die (Mark
14:36; John 18:11).

Inklings of understanding come when the context within
canonical scripture of Genesis 22 is made clear. Let us briefly
review that context.

The fateful drama of Abraham, Isaac, and God on Mount
Moriah takes place at a key juncture in the course of God's efforts, under way since Adam and Eve's temptation and fall, to
bring restoration and blessing to God's newly created world.
By Genesis 22, God has come up against frustration and heart-
break time and time again: in Cain's introducing murder into
the world, in the global proliferation of violence that led to

Noah's flood, and in the tower of Babel debacle, with its massive display of human hubris. In the wake of all this sin, God has been left rejected, alienated, boxed into a corner. There is a final course of action possible for God, but it is very unclear whether it is worth attempting it. That is where Genesis 22 comes in.

God's final recourse in setting creation back on track was appointing Abraham as a channel of God's glory and salvation. Since all direct outreaches to humanity had failed, God considered making Abraham and his progeny vicars of God, that is, living instruments of God's power-laden blessing. They could allow God to reach out to earth's people indirectly, working through a small subset of humanity. God could carefully nurture this group as intermediaries and first fruits.

The role emerges most clearly in Genesis 17:4–5, a few chapters before Isaac's near-sacrifice. God elevates Abraham as a spiritual "father" of nations. The appointment makes him a world spiritual leader on a par with King David, whom Isaiah 55:4 declares "a witness to the peoples, a leader and commander for the peoples."

God's final plan to reach out to the world involved granting Abraham the magnetic, royal glory of a vicar of God. It involved making him a channel of divine blessing powerful enough to attract the reverence of the nations. Exactly what is at stake in Abraham's role as a spiritual father of nations appears from a glance at Psalm 47:9. Here, the princes of earth assemble for worship specifically as "the people of the God of Abraham." How striking!

Abraham possessed a signal virtue crucial in order for God to use him in this plan: the virtue of "integrity." It is well worth elaborating on the nature of this virtue. It is a virtue shared by the Servant of the Lord of Second Isaiah.

In Hebrew thinking, integrity entails especially humility, transparency, and responsiveness before God. These core features are what permit one to reflect God's glory and honor to others. Putting on airs and displaying proud pretensions, in contrast, effectively block God's image from finding visible expression in people.[1]

Abraham's qualities of humility and vulnerability before God are prime reasons he caught the attention of Second Isaiah's writers. Isaiah's texts hold that God's power shines through such people. Isaiah 40:29 assures us that God "gives power to the faint, and strengthens the powerless." "Those who wait for the LORD shall renew their strength, they shall mount up with wings like eagles," echoes Isaiah 40:31.

Those with integrity may become vicars of God on earth, living channels for showing forth God's glory and saving power. Since the fate of the entire world hinges on the quality of integrity, God in Genesis 17:1 specifically commands Abraham to "walk before me with integrity" (translation mine). To do so means to adhere to God without reservations or conditions. Isaiah 38:3 expresses the same idea as Genesis 17:1, expressing it with the alternative language of following God with "wholehearted devotion" (cf. 1 Kings 9:4, NET/NIV).

Can Abraham, Sarah, and their people really be God's intermediaries to overcome the world's alienation from God? Can they be the means of blessing humanity as God always wanted? Only if they truly have the unique gift of integrity: the capacity to be wholly there for God, vulnerably present, walking before God even if that means taking the way of the cross. Staking everything on this gamble, God needs to have faith that Abraham can let go of self to let grace shine.

Having exhausted all other attempts at finding relationship with humanity, God is now risking the entire fate of the world on the family of Abraham and Sarah, hoping the couple can become spiritual beacons to the world. That is why God puts Abraham through the horrible test of Genesis 22. Deeply, grievously wounded (cf. Genesis 6:6), God must know if it is worthwhile attempting this final outreach to humanity. Does it have any chance of success? Apparently only if Abraham has integrity: the ability to transcend the self, to hold back nothing.

Only if Abraham is even able to commit to God the very future that God has promised both him and the world. Abraham must be that vulnerable, that capable of being wounded.

This, then, is the context in which God "tested" Abraham (Genesis 22:1), a context of examining whether true integrity and vulnerability are possible on earth. Just as Abraham proves cable of vulnerability, however, God does the same. God proves willing to accept, if necessary, the ultimate wound of permanent rejection by the world God has lovingly created. Endangering Isaac's life is a sure indication that God is laying absolutely everything on the line now. Isaac was the son of promise—the long-awaited child through whom God's everlasting blessing was to come to earth (Genesis 17:7).

Ellen F. Davis aptly summarizes all that is at stake for God in the great trial of Abraham's integrity in Genesis 22:

> God's first, direct approach to humanity did not
> work. So now God has chosen Abraham to be a
> kind of prism, catching the light of blessing and
> diffusing it into every corner of our sin-darkened
> world. Do you see, then, how dependent upon
> Abraham's faithfulness God now is? If Abraham
> goes his own way, if he tries to secure his own
> life apart from God's plan, then all God's hope of
> overcoming our evil is lost. If Abraham holds back
> anything at all from God, even the child Isaac, if
> Abraham is not wholehearted toward God, then the
> light of divine blessing cannot pass through him to
> bathe and reinvigorate our world. If Abraham is not
> wholehearted toward God, then it would be better
> if the world had never been made. That is what this
> terrible test is about.[2]

Even with this realization—the realization that a horribly wounded God must prove to God's self that human integrity on earth is possible—we recoil from Genesis 22 in shock and horror. How was Abraham able to obey the awful command to sacrifice his son? We are sure we would react differently. We would surely have resisted tooth and nail a divine command requiring this of us! Far from going up Mount Moriah willingly, as Abraham did, God's messengers would doubtless have needed to drag us up kicking and screaming.

Some among us could perhaps have mustered the courage to make the miserable trek, but only in profound resignation and despair. To walk this path of pain with Abraham would be to lose one's joy forever. What is striking is that Abraham undertook the offering of Isaac without the apparent despair we would expect. He forced himself to relinquish Isaac to God, but all the while apparently trusted that Isaac would not be lost. For modern Western Bible readers, comfortable in suburban lifestyles, Abraham's composure is completely disorienting.

Of all Genesis 22's interpreters, Kierkegaard perhaps best appreciated Abraham's spirit. In *Fear and Trembling*, he stood amazed before Abraham, whose humble courage allowed him to let go of Isaac, all the while believing that in so doing he would somehow receive back his son, his life's joy. Most of us do not know such radical, fearless trust today. It must come only as a gift of God—a miracle.

Abraham tells his servants, "We [*both* Isaac and I] will return to you" (Genesis 22:5, NJPS/The Tanakh 1985). He was somehow able to focus resolutely on the truth of God's promises, despite finding nothing of support to draw on from within normal human experience. The writer of Hebrews 11 grasped this well, though he went too far in putting conscious thoughts of resurrection in Abraham's head: "He who had received the promises was ready to offer up his only son, of whom he had been told, 'It is through Isaac that descendants shall be named for you.' He considered the fact that God is able even to raise someone from the dead" (Hebrews 11:17–19).

Rather than believing Abraham anachronistically possessed a conscious knowledge about Christian resurrection, we do better to think of him having a singular, riveted focus on God's goodness. He believed, despite all possible human calculation, that God would somehow not demand Isaac of him in the end or else would make things right in some other manner that only God could foresee—one that lay wholly outside the mundane, the everyday. The text practically shouts this truth.

When Isaac notices that he and his father lack a victim for their sacrifice, Abraham assures him, "God will provide for himself the lamb for the burnt offering, my son" (22:8). When Abraham chooses a name for Mount Moriah it is *Yahweh-Yireh*, "The LORD Provides," "The LORD sees to it" (22:14, NET/NASB). "Moriah" itself sounds like the Hebrew root for "provide" or "see to it." That root appears five times in the chapter, which is unusually frequent. All this is no coincidence; the whole story of Genesis 22 revolves around how God wondrously provides for God's people's deepest needs, seeing to it they are met. Abraham's God is the God who always provides.

Abraham believed God as he ascended Mount Moriah; yet Abraham suffered profoundly in his trek of faith. His extraordinary trust in God—his sure conviction that God, beyond all reasonable hope, would somehow provide for him and for Isaac—did not spare him one ounce of anguish at sacrificing his son. Abraham loved his son with all his soul. For a father so deeply attached to his child, the act of sacrificing him was an excruciating trauma.

Although Genesis 22 is traditionally called the "Near Sacrifice of Isaac"—or, in Jewish tradition, the "Binding of Isaac"—I believe that Abraham, Isaac's father, is the passage's true sacrificial offering. Scripture focuses on Abraham's ordeal, not that of Isaac. In fact, the passage offers little sense of Isaac's experience bound upon the altar in verse 9. Then, he essentially drops from the story. Verse 19 does not even mention Isaac returning home with Abraham.

While Isaac's experience is not the focus of our passage, Abraham's agony tugs at readers' hearts. Torn between love of God and love of his son, Abraham pours himself out on behalf of both parties as the story proceeds. We have seen that

Abraham's virtue of integrity means he follows God whole-heartedly. Abraham is completely there for God, immediately responding, "Here I am," when summoned (Genesis 22:1, 11). He is just as present for Isaac, repeating, "Here I am," when his son needs his reassurance (Genesis 22:7). These two wrenching pulls on Abraham almost tear him apart by the climax of the passage.

God knew the strength of Abraham's love for Isaac, referring to it with poetic intensity. At the start of the passage God piles up four different expressions identifying Isaac, each one express-ing more powerfully Abraham's attachment to his son: "Take now your son, your only son, whom you love, Isaac" (Genesis 22:2, NASB). The second of these expressions, "your only son" ("your *yakhid*") describes Isaac as unique, irreplaceable.

But there is more to this term, much more. The speakers of both Psalm 22:21 and Psalm 35:17 use the same expression (Hebrew: *yakhid*) to refer to their own dear lives, which they hold priceless. Abraham's sacrifice in Genesis 22 was the sacri-fice of his own dear life, his own being. In making this sacrifice, he became a model Suffering Servant of the Lord.

Other signs within the text betray the depth of Abraham's self-sacrifice. The Hebrew root behind "only son," for example, reappears in the adverb "together" in 22:6. Abraham and Isaac ascend Mount Moriah "together," united in love. While Isaac carries the wood of the offering, Abraham holds on to the flint and knife, keeping the dangerous implements well away from his son. Abraham's loving care for Isaac is nothing short of breathtaking.

A well-known 1655 etching by Rembrandt of Genesis 22 beautifully captures the suffering of Abraham in offering up his son. The scene captures the precise moment of the heavenly messenger's intervention in verse 11, interrupting the sacrifice. Abraham's emotional union with his son is apparent. With his right arm, he cradles Isaac's head, holding it gently near his lap. His fingers cover the lad's eyes, shielding them from the sight of the knife in his other hand. The focus of emotional passion in the etching, however, is Abraham's face. Looking closely, there emerges a haunting image of aged, tender frailty and deep, wrenching grief. Abraham's stricken countenance and blank stare reveal the cost to him of this experience—an ultimate cost.

Abraham models pure self-transcendence and other-centeredness. Rembrandt well expresses the text's presentation of Abraham as a sacrificial offering to God.

Rembrandt's etching reminds us of another biblical figure, Job, who faithfully endured unspeakable suffering. Job suffered "from the sole of his foot to the crown of his head" (Job 2:7). Exactly like Abraham, Job was truly "a man of integrity, and upright, who reveres God" (Job 1:8; cf. 1:1; 2:3, 9; 27:5; 31:6, translation mine). Through his ordeal, he proves to be a model for faithful living in a world of pain. What is more, he shows us how to love God with pure selflessness, purely for the sake of the beloved. Job loses everything—his herds, his family, his health—yet does not break off his relationship with God. He blames and rages at God, to be sure, but throughout his long time of pain persistently holds on to God.

Abraham's gift of other-centeredness gave God just the instrument needed to bring blessing to creation. At least, this was the understanding of the earliest interpretation of Abraham's trek up Mount Moriah. We find that interpretation in verses 15–19 of Genesis 22, which early biblical editors added to our account to help readers understand it.

In verses 15–19 of our chapter, there is a second discourse between the Lord's messenger and Abraham, separate from that in verses 11–12. Now, God explains to Abraham that his willingness to faithfully bear ultimate suffering has freed God's hands. It has given God a means of fulfilling God's plans and promises.

Abraham has just completely transcended his self, relinquishing everything to God, including his only son, his beloved son (v. 16). He has thereby demonstrated that he and his descendants who take up his calling are able to embrace the spiritual capacity of integrity. They have the capacity to be channels of God's power, through whom God can bless "all the nations of the earth" (v. 18). Though Abraham's trial was unique, v.18 is unambiguous that God's calling and empowerment pass from him to those who follow after him (Isaiah 59:21 picks up this theme). God's messenger declares to Abraham that earth's nations will gain their blessing "by your offspring."

This capacity of Abraham and his people—this pure model of selflessness—will prove a tremendous gift to all earth's peoples, which they may be able to mirror in some way. Abraham's unique, ultimate sacrifice is not intended for repetition by the rest of us—he is our spiritual champion, our knight of faith. His example, however, paves the way to a new, saving form of living for earth's people. Abraham is rightly known not only as a knight, but also as the *father* of the faith, a father with offspring.

The Servant Songs of Second Isaiah appear to have understood Abraham's sacrifice in just the way I have outlined. His humility and wholehearted trust in God provided the songs' authors a powerful key for sketching the character of the Lord's Suffering Servant. With some justification, one can speak of Abraham and the Servant in the same breath.

With Abraham as his model, the Servant is transparently loyal, God-enlightened, and completely calm. Like Abraham, he reveals the power of integrity and sacrificial love to represent God on earth. The Servant and Abraham are one in embodying the role of father, or parent, of the faith. They each work to birth a new community of vicars of God on earth.

In Isaiah 53, the Servant is transparently devoted to God, like a tender root growing up before the Lord (53:2). Although people consider his sufferings to be punishments, he is innocent of wrongdoing: "He had done no violence" (53:9).

Fascinatingly, the adjective for having integrity in Hebrew is the same term for an *unblemished* sacrifice (see Exodus 29:1;

Leviticus 1:3; 5:15). The Servant is an acceptable ritual offering, so he must necessarily have this ritual type of integrity. Other language in the poem reinforces this theme. When Isaiah 53:9 declares that "there was no deceit in his mouth," for example, there are strong connotations of ritual purity (see Isaiah 6:7).

The Servant of the Lord is transparent and humble (53:2; cf. Isaiah 42:3; 50:6). Indeed, being "despised" and "of no account" (Isaiah 53:3), he lacks all human ground for boasting. Unlike the proud with their gaping mouths, he has bridled his tongue (Isaiah 53:7). Because of his lowliness, God lifts him up, as two of the poem's verses stress. In Isaiah 53:12, God states, "I will allot him a portion with the great, and he shall divide spoil with the strong." More strongly, Isaiah 52:13 reads, "See, my servant shall prosper; he shall be high and lofty and greatly exalted" (translation mine).

The Servant of the Lord overturns everything. "He shall startle many nations; kings shall shut their mouths because of him (Isaiah 52:15). "Thus says the LORD, the Redeemer of Israel and his Holy One, to one deeply despised, abhorred by the nations, the slave of rulers, 'Kings shall see and stand up, princes . . . shall prostrate themselves, because of the LORD, who is faithful, the Holy One of Israel, who has chosen you'" (Isaiah 49:7).

I am convinced that Genesis 22 provides the primary model of suffering servanthood by which Isaiah's Servant of the Lord, and thus, ultimately, Jesus Christ, redeems creation and births a new form of human living on earth. The text presents us with a servant of God who startles the nations, turns the world upside down, and brings us God's atonement. No wonder this text has proved so central in both Judaism and Christianity. No wonder Professor Moberly was insistent at the Boston SBL that Professor Collins was abandoning this text as sub-Christian much too quickly.

When confronted with a difficult, offensive, or disturbing passage in scripture, the theologically responsible thing to do is to stay with the text and wrestle with it, closely studying its details and echoes of other scriptures. The history of its reception by synagogue and church may provide encouragement about its enduring value. Be attentive to its canonical context and shape, noting how it has been treated by its editors and by subsequent biblical writers. Above all, be open to its witness to transcendent reality. Be willing to side with Abraham in his focus on God's truth, a truth that may often appear to contradict all that we know from experience.

Notes

1   "Integrity" is not about a lack of sin, as a close reading of the psalms of lament can confirm (e.g., v. 4 and v. 12 of Psalm 41 are not contradictory). It has to do, rather, with transparency and responsiveness before God.

2   Ellen F. Davis, "Vulnerability, the Condition of Covenant," in *The Art of Reading Scripture* ed. E. F. Davis and R. B. Hays (Grand Rapids, MI: Eerdmans, 2003), 283.

Reading Race
in the New Testament:
Diversity and Unity

John Y. H. Yieh

The conspicuous inscription around the stained glass behind the altar of the VTS chapel—"Go ye into all the world and preach the gospel"—is a stout reminder of the mandate for which we gather on this Holy Hill in Alexandria to be prepared. It reminds us daily of the seminary's proud tradition of sending out missionaries to every corner of the world to preach God's love to the people living on many lands in its 190 years of history. This inscription is cited from a long ending of the Gospel of Mark, but the picture of Jesus standing on the hill often evokes the image of the risen Jesus charging his disciples "to make disciples of all nations, baptizing them in the name of the Father, and of the Son, and the Holy Spirit, and teaching them all that I have commanded" as reported in the great commission (Matthew 28:19–20). Indeed, a grand vision of triple mission: evangelize the world, baptize the believing, and teach the baptized, is vividly presented to summon us to serve the Lord in the wide world after we have worshiped, prayed, and celebrated the Eucharist in the chapel. The whole world should be visited and all the people—woman and man, rich and poor, free and oppressed, and in all colors—be evangelized, baptized, and taught, because they are all beloved children of God.

Living in a world that is ethnically multiple, culturally various, and socially diverse, how do we find a proper hermeneutic to read the scripture to hear what it has to say about the harsh reality of racial tensions, cultural conflicts, and economic disparities, both locally and globally, which confronts the promise of the gospel and its way of life? Taking social-cultural contexts seriously in reading the texts of the scripture for deeper understanding and proper appropriation is an important first step to serving our mission to preach the gospel in all the world. In Chinese painting and Japanese gardens, landscape is not merely a background for decoration but an integral part of its aesthetic entirety. Likewise, social-cultural contexts make an indispensable landscape for the meaning of texts, biblical and preached, and are indeed an essential part of the symbolic universe in which one thinks and behaves. It is in the ongoing interaction between biblical texts and life contexts that the presence and work of God are revealed. In order to explain God's presence and work to the world, therefore, it is imperative to appreciate the social-cultural landscape of the biblical world, and it is crucial to be able to tell the "signs of the time" in our life today. For this reason, ideological criticisms such as liberation-theological, feminist, and postcolonial interpretation, which bring current social realities into focus for us, are worthy of critical attention, as well as historical exegesis and theological expositions of biblical texts.

Clothe Yourselves with Christ

As the demography of the U.S. becomes diversified and the global village shrinks in size, racial-ethnic tensions, bonded with cultural, social, political, and economical conflicts, have become a focal point in the landscape of biblical interpretation and Christian ministry. What does the New Testament have to offer to disentangle these bundles of problems? The grand vision that Paul presented in Galatians 3:27–28 remains the shining goal of hope: "As many of you as were baptized into Christ have clothed yourselves with Christ. There is no longer Jew or Greek, there is no longer slave or free, there is no longer male and female; for all of you are one in Christ Jesus."

This statement arises from Paul's arguments with some Jewish Christian teachers, the so-called Judaizers, who want to impose Jewish cultural traditions on the Gentile Christians in Galatia, and it offers an ideal vision of Christian hope—equality and unity for all people in Christ. Living in society, one's "personhood" is defined by ethnic identity, economic status, and gender, so in this statement Paul recognizes the social-economic and gender-sexual as well as racial-cultural divides that separate one person from another, but he goes beyond the discrimination and hostility that such diversities often entail to affirm the "oneness" that all the baptized share in Christ. Those who have clothed themselves with Christ in baptism shall find affinity and unity with other Christians because they are all members of the same body of Christ, intimate and related. In Roman society, a person's ethnic identity, economic status, and gender are arranged in a hierarchical structure, from Roman male ruler to the Egyptian female slave. Each person has a specific location in the pyramid of power and dominance. Paul's vision subverts that pyramid structure. In Christ, he claims, every person, despite his or her ethnic identity, economic status, and gender, has equal worth before God and has a loving relationship with one another. They live in a concentric circle with Jesus Christ at the center. In order to regulate life and manage power, the Romans rank people and set up boundaries. With the baptism of repentance and transformation, however, Christ frees every person to live a new life and rearranges interpersonal relationships to build up a unified community. Symbiosis with diversities becomes the new model of life together. An alternative view of society is thus made possible by Christ, and the Church ought to live it out as a testimony to the world.

No Longer Jew or Greek

How does Paul the Pharisaic persecutor of early followers of Jesus become the Apostle to the Gentiles? How does Jesus, born the King of the Jews and who prohibits his followers from going to the Gentiles or the Samaritans, end up commissioning his disciples to make disciples of all nations? Several stories in the New Testament well illustrate how the issue of ethnic-cultural identity presents a serious social challenge and theological problem for early Christians and how it turns into a blessing for the Church Universal. One most critical and pressing question with tremendous social implications was: can Gentiles, idol worshipers, or violent colonizers be accepted as full members of the Church? Gentile proselytism was not simply a Judaic question that Rabbi Hillel and Rabbi Shammai were debating over in their separate schools. It took a vision of unclean animals from heaven in Joppa and a witness to the Holy Spirit descending on Cornelius in Caesarea to convince Peter that God shows no partiality but accepts in every nation anyone who fears him and does what is right (Acts 10:34–35). Even so, Peter felt the pressure to withdraw from the table with the Gentiles when the brothers from James arrived in Antioch (Galatians 2:12). Ethnic-cultural identity was also a Christian debate over which Paul and the Judaizers kept fighting in several churches (Galatians 3:1; Philippians 3:2) and which prompted the Apostles to meet in Jerusalem to find a settlement (Acts 15:6).

Why are ethnic-cultural differences so difficult to over-come? E. Shils, a British social anthropologist, defines ethnicity as rooted in common ties of kinship, shared territory, and shared tradition. Because "congruities of blood, speech, custom, (are seen to) have an ineffable, and at times overpowering coerciveness in and of themselves," it is difficult for anyone to think or move beyond the confinement of his or her own ethnicity.[1] Because we are so closely tied in one particular group of people as we grow up and undergo acculturation and socialization, we become who we are by our own habits. Every ethnic group develops a distinctive culture of its own. And culture, as defined by Clifford Geertz, is "a historically transmitted pattern of meanings embodied in symbols, a system of inherited conceptions expressed in symbolic forms by means of which —[its members] communicate, perpetuate, and develop their knowledge about and attitudes toward life."[2] Like others, Jewish people develop their own tradition of purity laws, holy days, and dietary rules which identify who they are and regulate what they do as an ethnic group. Their culture becomes their ethnic identity. Thus, it is very difficult to overcome one's own ethnic-cultural prejudice.

Because ethnicity entails culture as embodied in a set of symbols and practices sustained by their deep-rooted belief system, conversion of Gentiles also posed a theological question to the earliest Christians: how can it reconcile with the idea of the Jews as chosen people of God and God's promise to them? So, we hear Paul argue in earnest that all who believe are the descendents of Abraham in whom all the Gentiles shall be blessed (Galatians 3:7–8), and that by including the Gentiles, God does not break the promise of the covenant with Jewish people (Romans 9:6). In fact, God's righteousness is kept intact and even fulfilled, Paul contends, when God offers salvation to everyone who has faith, "to the Jew first and also to the Greek" (Romans 1:16, KJV). It is Christ and his cross that made it possible (Romans 3:21–26). Following Paul's argument, it is easy to understand why the author of Ephesians can say with boldness: "For he [Christ] is our peace; in his flesh he has made both groups [Jews and Gentiles] into one and has broken down the dividing wall, that is, the hostility between us . . . that he might create in himself one new humanity" (Ephesians 2:14–15). When and only when the "one new humanity" is created in Christ can Jewish Christians overcome their ethnocentric prejudice to say to the Gentile Christians, "So then you are no longer strangers and aliens, but you are citizens with the saints and also members of the household of God" (Ephesians 2:19). Ethnicity as a theological problem is thus solved by a theological argument on the basis of the amazing story of God's love in Christ, and it demands a transformation of mind and behavior that has social implications on racial-ethnic tensions and cultural conflicts.

One "scandalous" story that cuts very deep into the wounds of racial discrimination and cultural prejudice is the Canaanite woman who pleads for Jesus' help to save her daughter's life (Matthew 15:21–28). The disciples in disdain want to push this Gentile woman away and Jesus uses a racial slur ("dog") against her and her people (15:26) while privileging the Jews as "children of God" who deserve the food. How do we make sense of Jesus' cold attitude toward this persistent Gentile woman who seems to be bothering him? Perhaps Jesus means to emphasize that his mission before the crucifixion is to preach to the lost sheep of the house of Israel (15:24), or that he is exhausted and frustrated by the mounting oppositions against his ministry in Galilee (12:2, 10, 24; 14:3, 10; 15:2) and is now seeking personal retreat in the district of Tyre and Sidon (15:21). Jesus is apparently surprised by the Canaanite woman who, confident in her ethnic-cultural identity despite the racial slur, insists on her right to receive God's help saying that "even the dogs eat the crumbs that fall from their masters" (15:27). She demonstrates how the ethnically marginalized can claim by faith a seat at the table of God, whose inclusive love is open and inviting to all. In so doing, she helps Jesus hear God's voice in her persistent call, see her love for her daughter and her faith in him, and therefore change his mind to heal her daughter from a distance. In love that endures, miracle can happen. Ethnic tension and cultural clash are smoothed and healing takes place. In Matthew's view, this story prefigures the inclusion of the Gentiles in God's plan of salvation; thus, he reports how Jesus changes his mission mandate from going only to the lost sheep of the house of Israel (10:6; 15:24) to making disciples of "all nations" (28:19).

Besides the Canaanite woman, the centurion in Capernaum, who asks for healing on behalf of his servant, receives high praise from Jesus: "Truly I tell you, in no one in Israel have I found such faith" (Matthew 8:10). Another centurion at the cross confesses Jesus to be "truly God's Son" (Mark 15:39), while the Jewish on-lookers taunt the dying Jesus. Such high praises for the "model minorities" and "righteous Gentiles" reflect the reality of ethnic prejudice prevailing in the psyche of the public but also indicate how Jesus replaces ethnic preference with spiritual character as the criterion of receiving God's favor. Indeed, both the Gentiles and the Jews have fallen short of the glory of God and are in need of the grace of redemption in Christ (Romans 1–3). In the end, as the chosen people reject it, the Kingdom of God will be given to "a people (*ethnos*) that produces the fruits of the kingdom" (Matthew 21:43). The new people of God are defined by faithfulness and righteousness rather than ethnic lineage.

No Longer Slave or Free

Members of a racial-ethnic minority group can suffer from dis-crimination and self-doubt because they are socially disfran-chised and economically deprived by a majority group that con-trols social resources. It is no wonder that seeking to comfort his disciples upon his departure from the world, Jesus would say that he will call them "friends" and not "slaves" any longer (John 15:15), because slaves do not know what their master is doing, but Jesus has revealed everything to them about who he is and what he does. Calling them friends, he treats them as equals.

Indeed, change of social status means change of relationship, as is most evident when a slave is redeemed with a large sum of money to become a freedman who can then choose as a legal right where to work and whom to serve. Precisely because slaves enjoy no civil rights, it is remarkable that Paul would voluntarily call himself Christ's slave, willing to devote his life totally to serving the gospel and building up the Church. He does not claim freedom for himself anymore, but lives to serve Christ Jesus as his Lord. It demonstrates a complete dedication and genuine love for Jesus Christ.

The metaphorical use of slaves in these two cases is easily understandable, but the instruction in Ephesians 6:5–7 for the Christian slaves, who are almost certainly non-Romans, to stay willingly in their social rank and serve their masters sincerely as if serving Christ is difficult to accept from a slave's point of view and from a liberation theological perspective. All people are born equal to enjoy freedom and dignity. This birthright is what the biblical stories of Genesis, Exodus, and Amos have made explicit. The argument that their reward from God will be great sounds more like a concern to maintain the status quo for social order than an advocacy for the liberty of the oppressed (Ephesians 6:8), and it is true that much exhortation in Ephesians follows closely the conventional household codes of the Greek culture and Roman custom. It is possible, though, that the "slaves" in this passage might refer to the "servants" who are freemen or freed men for hire. They are urged to be conscientious workers in serving their masters so that their loyalty and good works may serve as praiseworthy witness to Christian faith. It is also important to note that the exhortation in Ephesians includes the duty of the masters to treat their servants or slaves kindly and fairly without threats, knowing that they have the same Master in heaven who is impartial in judgment. In other words, the author urges both slaves and masters, even though they belong to different social classes, to be mindful of the accountability before the just God in their dealing with each other.

Another well-known and difficult case is Paul's appeal in his letter to Philemon to receive the runaway slave Onesimus as a brother. In crafting this public letter to the Church to address Philemon on personal business, Paul successfully pleads the case for Onesimus. He makes an emotional appeal to Philemon based on their mutual love, affection, and indebtedness, and pressures him with the watchful eyes of the whole community to welcome Onesimus back no longer as a slave but as a beloved brother. He urges Philemon to make that decision based on the principle of Christian love rather than social convention or personal profit. So, a slave is freed, a master *absolves* some financial loss to testify to the virtue of Christian charity, and a community of faith is encouraged to practice love for one another. Some critics, however, find fault with Paul for not confronting the social institution of slavery as such. He may have saved one fortunate slave, they complain, but he has also condoned an evil system. Many philosophers in antiquity condemned slavery on moral grounds, even though they took no social or political actions to overthrow it, because slaves provided the necessary labor in the fields and in the cities to sustain the economic system and social service of the Roman Empire. One-third of the population in Rome was slaves, one-quarter in Italy, and one-tenth in major cities. In a pyramidal hierarchy, every social class, from the emperor, senators, governors, free citizens, freed men, to the slaves performs an assigned social function to keep peace and order. Hence, even those who consider slavery morally wrong are beneficiaries of this institution. This is what a structural evil can do: to choke the still voice of justice by dividing people into haves and have-nots and letting them fight each other. Is such social entanglement the reason why Paul did not condemn slavery? Is it simply too overwhelming? We do not know. Perhaps he was more concerned about individual slaves than the system of slavery. Perhaps he believed that the Lord would return soon to render universal justice, so it was not his immediate concern to reform the social economic systems of the world that lay under the authority of evil. It is clear, however, that Paul left behind an important legacy of love and reconciliation to help Christians make right moral choices, treating people, even those who have cost one material benefits, as brothers and sisters in Christ. A new community can be created when the division of social classes is overcome and debts are forgiven because of the love of Christ.

One might think also of the parable of the prodigal son in Luke 15:11–32. When the prodigal son returns home, he is welcomed back with a lavish feast. Even though he thinks he can only hope to work as a hired servant for food, the generous love of the father, surprising everyone, restores him to his original status as the son. The elder brother, on the other hand, has a hard time taking his brother back. Where is justice in such generosity to the unworthy? Indeed, it is not easy to treat someone deemed unworthy no longer as slave but free, and it is very difficult to reconcile with such a person as the father wishes for them to do, unless one can take the father's view.

How does the vision of "no longer slave or free" challenge us today? First of all, in the Church at the very least, social status and economic level should not divide the members as they do in a capitalist society where people are ranked and treated according to their wealth and power. CEOs and factory workers, professionals and new immigrants should be able to sit at the same table for Eucharist, for prayers, for Bible studies, and for coffee fellowship without discrimination. Until then, the household of God would remain divided and dysfunctional. Looking at the new world order where the G-7 economic superpowers reign, as postcolonial critics point out, the vision of "no longer slave or free" also challenges us to see what the so-called global economy designed by the rich countries is really doing to other peoples and other nations, especially formerly colonized countries in South America, Africa, and South Asia: cheap labor, child slaves, material exploitation, drug experimentation, toxic waste, and immigrant workers, except for a few government officials and trade-agents who are rewarded with individual wealth. Neo-colonial dominance and economic exploitation by

"Christian" nations from the Global North have fostered racial hatred, economic injustice, and extreme poverty among the vast population in the Global South. Conscientious Christians in the north should pay close attention to this development.

No Longer Male and Female

In the creation story of Genesis, God created Adam and Eve so they could keep company with each other to take care of the world. Man and woman are thus meant to love and support each other as equal partners in their daily lives. Unfortunately, gender relationships between man and woman or husband and wife can deteriorate into dominating, exploitative, and abusive relationships for personal, social, and economic reasons. Gender injustice often results in domestic violence, broken marriages, and dysfunctional families. Individual personality and moral character are certainly responsible in many cases, but the prevailing patriarchal conventions and *kyriarchal* (imperial) systems have the lion's share of the blame because they create an environment in which gender injustice is perpetuated from generation to generation.

It is true that, even though some women supporters of Jesus' ministry are named (Luke 8:2–3), their inquiry and response to Jesus were exemplary (John 4:7; 11:20), their love and courage in tending Jesus' body and tomb (Mark 15:40; 16:1) and witness to Jesus' resurrection (Mark 16:9) are reported, the Evangelists manage to forget the name of the woman anointing Jesus' head with nard, whom Jesus specifically said should be remembered wherever the gospel is proclaimed (Mark 14:9; Matthew 26:13). Paul did have woman co-workers in ministry, such as Lydia, Priscilla, and Phoebe, but he also said the husband is the head of his wife and tried to silence some women preachers in Corinth (1 Corinthians 11:2–16; 14:34–36). It is worth noting that he did suggest that women can pray and prophesy (11:5) and emphasized that "Nevertheless, in the Lord woman is not independent of man or man independent of woman. For just as woman came from man, so man comes through woman; but all things come from God" (11:11–12).

Often controversial is the *Haustafel* instruction of Ephesians 5:21–6:4. Since the household is considered a basic unit and microcosm of society, its stability is the foundation of a peaceful and prosperous society, and the household codes that regulate the duties, obligations, and relationships of every member have profound social consequences. The author holds a high view of marriage, comparing the nuptial love of husband and wife to the divine love God has for the people. A wife is asked to be submissive to her husband, but the husband is asked to give his life for her as Christ died for the church. It is a reciprocal relationship. In fact, that is how the author begins the pericope: "Be subject to one another out of reverence for Christ" (5:21), and this principle governs the exhortation both to wife (5:22) and to husband (5:25). Also noteworthy is that Genesis 2:24, "For this reason a man will leave his father and mother and be joined to his wife, and the two will become one flesh," is cited to emphasize the complete "union" of the two in matrimony (Ephesians 5:31). Judging from these examples, the early Church may have developed relatively more liberating views on gender relationship than the cultural norms of the time, but it also continued to wrestle with specific gender issues.

Elisabeth Schüssler Fiorenza finds most intolerable the patriarchal prejudice assumed in the history of interpretation and deeply embedded in biblical narratives and biblical ideas, which have been used to legitimate and reinforce social discrimination against women. She also detests what she calls the kyriarchal domination, inscribed in biblical language and text, which has not only corrupted every level of the church's hierarchy but has also contributed to the brutally oppressive political-social-economical systems on a global scale. This is why gender justice is also related to reading race in the New Testament. To her, the two hard rocks that obstruct gender justice and human liberty are the power-seizing ideologies of male-centered patriarchy (evident in chauvinism in many cultures) and empire-building kyriarchy (exemplified in Pax Romana and Pax Americana), both of which sustain the initial creation and continuous interpretation of the Bible. Harboring both ideologies, the Bible becomes a potent tool with which men and empires (including the Church) consolidate their power to dominate women and colonize others by means of violent language, abusive ethos, political systems, social structures, and military might. Used in this way, the Bible functions as a political text. A faithful reader of the Bible can internalize the androcentric presupposition and kyriarchal rhetoric so deeply that his or her interpretive imagination and ethical values are totally conditioned by these ideologies.

In order to "detoxify" these suppressive ideologies, which have been inextricably woven into the fabric of the Bible and to "conscientize" the readers, Schüssler Fiorenza calls for a complete transformation of the discipline of biblical studies. In *The Power of the Word*, she proposes a "transnational decolonizing interpretation" to articulate a "radical democratic religious imaginary" by engaging a critical task in three dimensions: historical *redistribution*, ideological *deconstruction*, and ethical—political as well as religious—theological constructive *representation*. By "radical democratic religious imaginary" she means that the "ekklēsia of women" should offer new "language and space for the imagination to develop a public religious discourse," and in that discourse "justice, participation, difference, freedom, equality and solidarity set the ethical conditions."[3] The three dimensions to be articulated can be perceived as an interpretive strategy in three stages. The first stage, historical redistribution, is to employ a "hermeneutics of suspicion" in reading biblical texts to reconstruct a history of women in order to hear their hushed voices and rediscover their leadership and contributions. The second task, ideological deconstruction, is to use what she calls the "dance of interpretation" which involves seven hermeneutical reflections on experience, domination, suspicion, critical evaluation, memory and remembering, imagination, and transformation, so that the androcentric and kyriocentric ideologies in the Bible may be debunked. The third and final task, ethical theological constructive re-presentation, is to connect the emancipative imaginary of scripture to contemporary global struggles in order to "envision alternatives to those of all kinds of fundamentalisms, as well as encourage and empower women today for living well in the daily insecurity and violence of global empire."[4] Schüssler Fiorenza's ideological critique against the structural evil as embodied in racial, social, and gender injustice and her passionate advocacy for a theological and ethical interpretation of scripture to transform individual and social lives need to be carefully heeded.

One in Christ

As we reflect on Paul's vision of unity in Christ, it is sad to see that it remains a dream unrealized. In the Church as in the workplace, we still see individual and institutional racism, social and economic discrimination, and gender disparity hurting lives and relationships. Those who have clothed themselves with Christ in baptism should be able to live together in unity, and in doing so demonstrate the power of the new life in Christ that will change the world. Unfortunately, this remains a goal to be reached. What can be done, then, to assist us in pursuing that goal? Three metaphors for the Church in the New Testament may be helpful.

1. Branches and the vine. Before Jesus departs from the world, he prays for the unity of the disciples because the bond of love and support will help them endure suffering and hostility from a world that hates them. Jesus begins by saying, "I am the vine; you are the branches. Those who abide in me and I in them bear much fruit, because apart from me you can do nothing"

(John 15:5). It is not easy to overcome natural and human-made boundaries that separate one person from another, because everyone wants to survive and thrive in the society. Only when the branches are organically connected with the vine can they receive nutrients to grow and bear fruit. Thus it is by maintaining an intimate relationship with Jesus Christ our Lord who has given up his life to tear down the dividing wall which separates us from God and from one another that we will be able to love others as ourselves and become one with each other in Christ.

2.   The body of Christ. When the Corinthian church finds itself engulfed in factional fighting, liturgical misconduct, and conflict over spiritual gifts, Paul reminds them that the Church is the body of Christ and that they are all members of the same body. "There are varieties of gifts, but the same Spirit; and there are varieties of services, but the same Lord; and there are varieties of activities, but it is the same God who activates all of them in everyone" (1 Corinthians 12:4–6). We are the body of Christ and individually members of the body, so no one can say that he has no need of others. It is imperative to recognize that Christ alone is the head of the church, and we all need "others" to make a healthy body of Christ. In this metaphor, we also learn that it is in equality we seek to unify the diversities. There is no need to do away with diversity or impose uniformity. Instead, we can benefit from the diversity of gifts if only we honor each other with equality. In the body of Christ, all are gifts of God and all are needed.

3.   A holy temple in the Lord. One more metaphor for the church is noteworthy. When the author of Ephesians vehemently argues how Christ by his blood on the cross has made two groups of people, the Jews and the Gentiles, into one new humanity to make peace

between them and to reconcile both groups to God, he ends the pericope saying, "In him [Christ as the cornerstone] the whole structure is joined together and grows into a holy temple in the Lord; in whom you also are built together spiritually [or in the Spirit] into a dwelling place for God" (Ephesians 2:21–22). We are parts of the holy temple of God just as we are parts of the body of Christ. We each are indeed different in racial, social, and gender terms, but we are all essential and precious parts of the whole that may bring glory to God. The unity in Christ has an ultimate goal, that is, to become a glorious "place" where the holy God will be pleased to dwell and people may witness and worship God.

These metaphors are only some examples from the rich resources in the New Testament that illustrate how the unity of all people across racial-cultural, social-economic, and gender divisions may be conceived and achieved in Christ. At this critical time when our beloved church is facing controversies and schisms, if we want to live a life worthy of the calling to bear witness to the oneness in Christ, we surely need to "with all humility and gentleness, with patience, bearing with one another in love, making every effort to maintain the unity of the Spirit in the bond of peace" (Ephesians 4:1–3).

Notes

1   Edward Shils, "Primordial, Personal, Sacred and Civil Ties," *British Journal of Sociology* 8 (1957), 130–145. Cited in Mark C. Brett, *Ethnicity and the Bible* (Leiden: Brill, 1996), 12.

2   Clifford Geertz, *The Interpretation of Cultures* (New York: Basic Books, 1973), 89.

3   Elisabeth Schüssler Fiorenza, *The Power of the Word* (Minneapolis: Fortress Press, 2007), 29.

4   Schüssler Fiorenza, 33.

Don't Forget to Remember: Identity in Deuteronomy and Ruth

Judy Fentress Williams

broadcast of *Speaking of Faith* entitled "Alzheimer's, Memory and Being" featured a psychologist who led a writing workshop for patients in the early stages of Alzheimer's disease. Part of what makes this disease so terrifying is the loss of the individual that accompanies the loss of memory. When sufferers of Alzheimer's lose their ability to maintain connections to people, places, and events, they lose a part of who they are. This loss is shared by the community. Participants of the workshop were encouraged to write down a memory to share and thereby preserve it. The act of recalling the past in the presence of aggressive memory loss led to the observation that remembering "is always a creative process."[1]

That memory is a creative process is not simply the case for those suffering from severe memory loss. Forgetfulness is simply a part of the human condition. Despite our best efforts, we cannot hold onto everything we take in. In response to forgetfulness, we assemble memory from what we retain. As a result, our memories are inherently incomplete.

The shaping of memory is influenced not only by forgetfulness, but by our choices. In the telling of our stories and the shaping of our identities, we choose some components of our past over others. We tend to focus on our successes and strengths in the formation of our "official," public identities, and leave out the "unofficial" stories, those of our failures and shortcomings. Some aspects of our story are too painful to recall. Some elements of our past are "suitable" for one audience but deemed "unsuitable" for another. In other words, our memories are faulty by nature and selective by choice, which means we have faulty and selective identities.

Scripture is a corrective to our tendency towards forgetful and selective storytelling because it includes both the official and unofficial voices. Traditions, the parts of the story we uphold for others to see, sit alongside counter-traditions, those aspects of our identity that we sometimes prefer to leave out. These different types of memory form a dialogue around, other things, Israel's identity. In fact, Deuteronomy commands the people to maintain an identity that includes their experience in the wilderness. Deuteronomy's command then directs Israel and her children to remember their story as one that includes homelessness, wandering, and uncertainty.

Narrative and Identity in Deuteronomy

The book of Deuteronomy is a long narrative sermon perched on the edge of promise. As the last book of the Torah, it provides a conclusion to this first division of the Bible while setting the stage for the second division, the Prophets. In the canon, it functions as a "swing book," permanently occupying liminal space. Geographically, Deuteronomy takes place on the border between the wilderness and the land of promise. With the exception of the account of Moses' death, Deuteronomy adds little to the overall narrative of the Torah. This book is a narrative and geographical pause, a moment poised between the action of wandering in the wilderness and the action of entering Canaan. Moses tells Israel her story at this particular moment and in this place because it is central to her formation and identity as a people.

The command to remember is in tension with the human tendency to forget.

While in the wilderness, Israel's memory was faulty. The people's story was filled with incidents of forgetting the commands or forgetting to keep them. When Israel enters the land of promise, she will go from being a sojourner (*ger*) to a nation, a people of the land. In anticipation of this transition, Moses recounts the history of Israel in the wilderness. The sermonic history of Deuteronomy is filled with the commands to "Hear," "Take care," "Don't forget," and "Remember." The repetition of these commands assumes a faulty memory.

A closer examination of Moses' command to remember reveals a call to a specific memory. Moses wants Israel to take the memory of the wilderness into the land of promise. This is a rather peculiar request. One would imagine that after forty years of struggle in the wilderness, the people would like nothing more than to forget this difficult past. Yet, Moses' sermon makes numerous references to the people's experience in the wilderness as they prepare to leave it (Deuteronomy 6:10–12; 8:1–6; 9:6–29). The lessons of the desert are a part of the story that must not be lost in the potential prosperity of the Promised Land.

Ironically, Deuteronomy, the very book in which these instructions are recorded, is likely the lost and forgotten scroll referred to in 2 Kings 22:8–10. When Josiah read the book that was found in the Temple, he wept upon realizing what had been forgotten. Without the book, his people had forgotten rules that were central to their identity as God's people. The recovery of the book led to a massive reform (2 Kings 23:1–25).

As the story of Josiah and the lost book illustrates, memory is key to identity. Regina Schwartz goes further to say that in scripture, the ability to remember or recover what has been forgotten or lost is key to survival. She connects the pattern of remembering and forgetting in the Bible to the act of interpretation. Interpretation is "depicted as an activity of repressing and reconstructing, of forgetting and remembering and that activity, by its very nature resists completion."[2]

Remembering the wilderness protects against a history and identity based only on victories and moments of strength. If the wilderness experience is used to inform Israel's identity, Israel becomes, among other things, vulnerable, disobedient, willful, and afraid. In the wilderness she is utterly dependent upon God. There Israel experiences God's provision, protection, and guidance. For the narrative found in the book of Deuteronomy, forgetting the wilderness would mean forgetting the faithfulness of God.

The command to remember in Deuteronomy is tied to the command to teach, tell, and repeat Israel's story. This telling and retelling is not intended to happen in a vacuum; rather, Israel is commanded to tell the story to her children so that they can tell the story. As the children hear and then tell the story, they make it their own. By repeating the shared story, each person finds his or her place in the history and in the community. Israel's ability to keep this commandment—the remembering, retelling, and repetition of the Exodus sojourn in the wilderness and the entry to the Promised Land—transforms the historical event. The events of redemption and sojourn towards home are retold and interpreted and become literary motif. These are the dominant rubrics used by Israel to tell a story. The stories of the ancestors are stories of journey towards home. In the wilderness and in exile, Israel longs for home.

Narrative and Identity in Ruth

With the Deuteronomistic command to remember as a background, I want to examine Israel's story of Ruth. Ruth is one of the best-known and often-repeated stories of the Hebrew Bible. This short book contains the elements of loss and recovery—famine and harvest, barrenness and fruitfulness, life and death—requiring the characters in the narrative to interpret their context in order to establish or maintain an identity. It is an official and unofficial story about identity. It is official in that it concludes with a brief genealogy that leads to King David. It is unofficial because the main characters are women (Naomi and Ruth), they are widows, and Ruth is a Moabite. Thus Ruth provides a model for remembering a story so that one's identity is informed by weakness and strength, victory and failure. For the women in this story, interpretation is an act of survival. Against a changing backdrop, they repeat or interpret their story, and that allows them to define and redefine their identity, and in so doing come to understand the core values that constitute one's place in a community.

The story of Ruth uses two motifs to explore identity: the journey towards home and redemption. Israel's identity is based on the call and promise that included a homeland. Like the Israelites on the verge of entering Canaan, the shifts recounted in the narrative from the book of Ruth require the characters to interpret and reinterpret their context in order to establish and maintain an identity. In this story, the reader is invited to explore the issues of identity when the constructs that traditionally inform identity are missing.

The book of Ruth appears in the third division of the Hebrew Bible, Ketuvim. The book of Ruth is associated with the celebration of Shevu'ot, the feast of weeks.[3] The Septuagint placed Ruth in the second division of the Bible, *nevi'im*, or prophets, immediately after the book of Judges, because the book begins with the phrase, "In the days that the judges ruled . . . ." However, the language in Ruth suggests a later date than Judges. Another possibility is that Ruth was written as a response to the strident prohibition against intermarriage as recorded in Ezra and Nehemiah. Thus Ruth occupies different places in the canon and is associated with celebration or festival, judges and the period of time preceding the monarchy, and the post-exilic period of Ezra and Nehemiah. By its various placements, Ruth has a number of external dialogue partners.

Ruth is full of dialogue. The majority of the book of Ruth (fifty-five of the eighty-five verses) is made up of direct speech. This dialogue in Ruth does more than advance the plot of the narrative. The series of exchanges between Naomi, Ruth, Orpah, Boaz, and the people of Bethlehem are all connected by the theme of identity. For the women in this story, establishing identity is an act of survival. It is a performance, a demonstration of the way interpretation is life-giving.

The series of dialogues involving Ruth, Naomi, and Boaz demonstrates that their identities, their status or place in society, are affected by the encounter or dialogue with the other characters. Because dialogue expands the horizon of the individual, the dialogue forms bridges across the constructs that usually determine identity. The dialogues allow us to chart the shift in Ruth's identity from outsider to a respected and honored member of the family.

The first dialogic exchange is the best known of the dialogues in the book of Ruth. Verses 1 through 6 of chapter 1 provide the setting. Elimelech and his family, Naomi, Mahlon, and Chilion, leave Bethlehem because of a famine and sojourn to Moab. Elimelech dies in the land of Moab, and Naomi is left with her sons, who marry Moabite women, Orpah and Ruth. After a period of time (ten years), Mahlon and Chilion die. Naomi and her daughters-in-law are left behind. Around this time, Naomi receives word that the famine in Bethlehem is over, and she starts off for Bethlehem with her daughters-in-law. All of this information comes to the reader through the narrator. In these few verses, the narrator not only gives a summary of the action in the plot, but also exposes the constructs under which identity is formed in these societies. In this society women have restricted movement. They are daughters, wives, mothers, mothers-in-law, daughters-in-law, and widows. In other words, they are bound to and dependent upon the men in their families. The narrative also reveals that there are Israelites and there are others, in this case, Moabites.

In verse 7, Naomi and her daughters-in-law were "on their way to go back to the land of Judah." It is after she embarks on the return that Naomi orders her daughters to do the same, to go back to their homes, to their "mother's house." Both daughters-in-law resist and assert that they will go back with Naomi, to her people. Here Naomi reasons with them, speaking the refrain, "Turn back," reminding them that she has no other sons and the prospects of their procuring husbands is slim. For them to return with her is unreasonable because she has nothing to offer them. Naomi's argument is based on the existing constructs that shape identity in this culture. All three of them are widows, which makes them vulnerable. That her daughters-in-law are foreigners exacerbates the situation.

This dialogue is marked by the repetition of the verb *sub*, which is translated as "go back," "turn back," and "return." This word is replete with meaning. For the audience that heard this story in or after the exile, the word *sub* characterized the desire to return home from the place of exile.

The location of this dialogue is significant. Naomi is on her way back home with her daughters-in-law. After the journey is begun, Naomi pauses, almost as an afterthought. It is as if they have gone as far as they can together—in a literary sense, they have come to the end of what the societal constructs can allow for them. Moabite widows do not belong in Bethlehem, and as the women approached Bethlehem, it may have become evident to Naomi that in this other location, her daughters-in-law would take on an identity that would be a hindrance. They are at a crossroads.

Orpah sees the logic of Naomi's argument and, after weeping, kisses her mother-in-law goodbye. Ruth, however, does not let go, and so Naomi attempts to convince her again, this time pointing out that Orpah has gone back and that she should as well. Verses 16–17 record Ruth's response to Naomi's plea.

> Do not press me to leave you
> or to *turn back* from following you!
> Where you go, I will go;
> Where you lodge, I will lodge;
> your people shall be my people,
> and your God my God.
> Where you die, I will die—
> there will I be buried.
> May the LORD do thus and so to me,
> and more as well,
> if even death parts me from you!

Ruth's response to Naomi consists of five sets of doublets or parallel lines that end in a vow. The doublets have these words pairs: *leave/turn back, go/lodge, people/God, die/buried.* The first doublet is a negative command; the following three are a declaration. These three doublets in the middle intentionally place Naomi (you) first. The language reflects the force of the statement. Naomi will be followed by Ruth. Ruth is bound to Naomi. The dialogue ends with Ruth's words. The narrator tells us that Naomi said nothing in response to Ruth's words because "she saw that she was determined to go with her."

Ruth's words supply a response to Naomi's argument, albeit an unreasonable one. Ruth clings to Naomi out of loyalty. She makes the decision that her future and fate will be tied to Naomi, Naomi's people, and Naomi's God. In this exchange, Ruth's words tell us that identity is shaped by more than one's location and nationality, but by one's choices. Ruth chooses an identity that is based on faithfulness, *hesed.*

Prior to this moment, the women were brought together by circumstances of famine and marriage. Now Ruth makes an intentional commitment, evoking the language of covenant.

They have reached the limits of where they can go with their current identities, so Ruth attaches her identity to Naomi. She understands that if they are to continue on together, their current identities must be surrendered or altered. The language of covenant is intentional. The covenant is the bond that holds together another unlikely pair, namely God and God's people. It is God's persistence and faithfulness that have allowed Israel to continue.

The encounter between Ruth and Naomi evokes the setting for the book of Deuteronomy. Naomi is poised to return home to the land of promise in much the same way the children of Israel were prepared to enter this land once known as Canaan. Moses asks the people to take the memory of the wilderness with them, and Ruth asks Naomi to take her, a vivid reminder to Naomi of her loss, her childlessness, and her recent past as a sojourner. If Naomi allows Ruth to accompany her, she will be fundamentally altered. Similarly, Ruth's words demonstrate her understanding that her choice to stay with Naomi will require a shift in her identity.

In choosing to stay with Naomi, Ruth is doing more than choosing a new identity. Her words demonstrate a new construct for her identity. From now on, faithfulness, not ethnic background or husband, will be the construct that will inform identity. Ruth's faithfulness makes her vulnerable, and it is countercultural, but it is also the basis upon which the characters' lives are transformed.

With dialogue, the potential action of the story is multiplied. New constructs can come into being through dialogue, with endless possibilities. The work of dialogue always holds the potential for us to envision new worlds through those with whom we are engaged in dialogue, but this exchange demands something of us. The act of dialogue demands a certain level of vulnerability if we are to be open to one another. The vulnerability required of authentic dialogue makes possible the transformation that can take place across societal constructs.

In the narrative that follows her decision to stay with Naomi, Ruth's faithfulness is the primary factor that determines her identity. Ruth's faithfulness gets the attention of the redeemer Boaz, and she is rewarded with a family (husband and son) that provides stability for her and Naomi. It should be noted that Ruth's faithfulness is directed towards a purpose that is larger than her own circumstances. Ruth is praised as being worth more to Naomi "than seven sons." The child she bears is placed on Naomi's breast and is her heir. The narrative then shifts to give the genealogy that leads to David, son of Jesse. Ruth's faithfulness is the deciding factor in a story of national importance. That means, ultimately, the book of Ruth is not about Ruth, but the work of God.

In this first chapter of Ruth, we observe two journeys. The first is the one undertaken by Elimelech and his family as they leave their home in search of food. This first journey involves leaving the place to which their identity is rooted. While they are sojourners in Moab, Naomi's sons marry Moabite women. Intermarriage is counter to their identity as Israelites. Finally, Naomi's husband and sons die, and she and these Moabite daughters-in-law lose a primary indicator of identity, the men who inherit on their behalf and provide for them. This first journey is one in which identity based on homeland, marriage within one's people (for the sons), and marriage (for the women) is lost.

Naomi embarks on a second journey when there is food in her homeland, but she returns barren, stripped of the things around which her identity was built. When she attempts to send her daughters-in-law back, Ruth clings to her and, in so doing, forms a new basis for identity. Chapter 1:14 states, "but Ruth clung to her." The word here for clung, *dabaq*, is used to describe the union of a husband and wife in Genesis 2:24. Here the very vocabulary demands a new understanding of words associated with traditional constructs. In other words, the narrator uses a word traditionally associated with a woman and a man in marriage to describe Ruth's bond with Naomi. Ruth will remain with Naomi because of faithfulness, and this act will set into motion a course of events that will result in their redemption.

This shift is accomplished through dialogue. Ruth responds to Naomi's command to leave with a new construct of faithfulness that exceeds cultural constraints. The dialogue in this chapter and throughout the narrative explores the existing constructs of identity over and against the faithfulness of Ruth. Ruth's faithfulness represents God's faithfulness to Israel in the wilderness. God's faithfulness, like that of Ruth, is not bound by the cultural constructs of location, nationality, or gender. It is the core, ongoing value of Israel's identity.

Ruth's decision to stay with Naomi demands an adjustment of identity on the part of Naomi, as does the return home. Upon the women's return to Bethlehem, the townspeople take notice of Naomi and Ruth. The women said, "Is this Naomi?" to which she responded:

> Call me no longer Naomi,
> call me Mara,
> for the Almighty has dealt bitterly with me.
> I went away full,
> but the LORD has brought me back empty;
> why call me Naomi
> when the LORD has dealt harshly with me,
> and the Almighty has brought calamity upon me?
> (1:20–21)

In this dialogue, the women of Bethlehem raise a question about Naomi's identity. We know that while she was away from home, Naomi lost that part of her identity tied to her husband and her sons. What is not clear in the text is the basis for the women of Bethlehem's lack of recognition. Is it her widow's attire? Does she bear the effects of the famine? Is it simply the passage of time or is it the presence of the strange young widow who accompanies her? What is clear is that Naomi chooses a name that reflects her state of bitterness, *Mara*. This name forms a dialogue with Exodus 15:22–27, the account of the bitter waters the Israelites encounter after leaving Egypt.

In the Exodus narrative, the people are without water. After following Moses in the wilderness, they come to bitter water, which is appropriately called *Marah* (15:23). What is of interest in this narrative is that the people are led by God to the bitter waters of Marah, and after making the water drinkable, God sets the rules for their relationship. In Exodus 15:26, God says, "If you will listen carefully to the voice of the LORD your God, and do what is right in his sight, and give heed to his commandments and keep all his statutes, I will not bring upon you any of the diseases that I brought upon the Egyptians; for I am the LORD who heals you." In Exodus, God sets the terms for relating to Israel against the backdrop of blessing versus plague, water versus wilderness. It is a liminal moment. Similarly, the reference to Mara in Ruth acknowledges the fact that although Naomi has returned home, her identity is not certain and her future is not secure. When her identity is questioned by those who knew her years ago, she embraces the identity of loss. The identity of loss is only one part of Naomi's story. What is not reflected in her response (because she does not know this) is the possibility that exists in and through the faithfulness of the Moabite widow by her side.

The dialogue around identity (in changing situations) is raised in the next chapter where a series of exchanges occurs. The first and last exchanges in the chapter are between Ruth and Naomi (2:2; 2:19–22). In the first, Ruth informs Naomi that she intends to glean and Naomi affirms her wish. In the concluding dialogue in this chapter, Ruth reports to Naomi about her successful endeavor and her fortuitous encounter with Boaz, who, as "luck" would have it (v. 3), is a relative. These exchanges form an envelope around the two encounters between Ruth and Boaz. In verse 5, Boaz notices Ruth among the gleaners and asks, "To whom does this young woman belong?" The question is one of identity. Ruth's identity is tied to the person to whom she belongs. The response is, "She is the Moabite who came back with Naomi from the land of Moab" (v. 6). Ruth belongs to the land of Moab and Naomi. Armed with this information, Boaz speaks to Ruth directly, telling her where to glean and allowing her some privileges afforded his workers. Boaz's instructions create another shift in her identity. She is a gleaner who is to be treated like one of Boaz's workers. In response to his generosity, Ruth asks, "Why have I found favor in your sight, that you should take notice of me, when I am a foreigner?" (v. 10).

Boaz's response provides us with direction: "All that you have done for your mother-in-law since the death of your husband has been fully told me, and how you left your father and mother and your native land and came to a people that you did not know before. May the LORD reward you for your deeds, and may you have a full reward from the LORD, the God of Israel, under whose wings you have come for refuge! (vv. 11–12).

Boaz's treatment of Ruth does not make sense based on her national identity. For Boaz, the key to determining her identity at this point is Ruth's *hesed*, or faithfulness, to her mother-in-law. Faithfulness, the basis upon which Ruth is tied to Naomi in chapter 1, is the same basis upon which Boaz extends kindness to the Moabite widow in chapter 2. Boaz calls her "daughter" (2:8), which conveys kindness and may also speak to the difference in their ages.

Chapter 3 has three exchanges that continue the dialogue around identity. The first and the third are between Ruth and Naomi and the second is between Ruth and Boaz. As was the case in the preceding chapter, the first and third dialogues form bookends around the central exchange, where the course of Ruth's future status and identity will be determined. Here the nature of the dialogue takes a decisive turn. If in the first two chapters, identity is questioned or named; in the final two chapters, dialogue is used to ensure that this new identity or status is realized.

First Naomi instructs Ruth out of the need to secure their future. Naomi speaks in verses 1–4, giving Ruth a series of instructions on what she is to do on the threshing floor. Ruth simply responds, "All that you tell me I will do" (v. 5). Unlike the first exchange in chapter 1 (vv. 15–18) in which Naomi tells Ruth to return or go back, Ruth does not resist Naomi's instruction. Once the covenant has been made, the two work as a team, as evidenced in chapter 2. When Naomi shares her plan for their survival, Ruth complies and is willing to follow Naomi's plan as well as Boaz's commands. As Ruth follows Naomi's and Boaz's commands, the language of family is evoked. Both Naomi and Boaz refer to Ruth as "daughter," and both of them, up until this point in the narrative, exercise a parental role. Naomi and Boaz are related but not by marriage. The only way Ruth, the daughter, will be related to either of them is by marriage, a covenant. In following Naomi's and Boaz's direction, she becomes the wife of Boaz and the mother of Obed, who then is associated with Naomi. The identification of the child with Naomi may be an attempt to secure the child's Judaic lineage.[4] The child's name, *Obed*, means "he who serves." This child of Ruth, Boaz, and Naomi serves a number of purposes. The child born to Ruth and identified with Naomi takes away the stigma of loss to the one who called herself Mara. Moreover, the child's name also reflects his and his mother's role in the movement of this narrative. Ruth's faithful service restores the family line.

At each turn in the narrative of Ruth, the shifts in identity are conveyed by using more than one voice. It may be the expectation of a reader to have an omniscient narrator, but one voice is not adequate to the task. In this narrative, the dialogue takes the lead, and the dialogue is by nature unpredictable. By encountering a chorus instead of one official voice, the reader is given a fuller understanding of the story and is able to explore the complexity of identity. When we tell our story using more than one voice, we do a better job of remembering. Beyond the official or dominant story, there are the perspectives of the community that come from the margins. The stories of these members are often the stories of the wilderness: those of homelessness and disenfranchisement. The command in Deuteronomy to remember the story of the wilderness is honored in the Ruth narrative because the Moabite is allowed to speak. When the Moabite speaks, the ensuing dialogue allows her to move from "other" to daughter to wife, mother, and honored ancestor.

In this essay, I have formed an intentional dialogue between Deuteronomy and Ruth. Starting with Deuteronomy's unique command to remember as central to identity, I have then examined the dialogue in Ruth to glean directives for the creation of our own narratives in our communities of faith. The book of Ruth presents us with a narrative that contains both official and unofficial elements. These elements are held together with dialogue. Dialogue allows for a vision of identity that exceeds the traditional cultural constructs of identity. For contemporary communities of faith, the following observations can be made:

- *Deuteronomy reminds us that our shared story of identity should contain official and unofficial elements.* Deuteronomy's command is against our tendency to present our stories through a single, official lens. The unofficial parts of our story are often the places where the work of redemption takes place. God works through and in spite of our shortcomings and our failures. When we eliminate the unofficial elements of our story, we run the risk of establishing a false identity—one that is not based on the faithfulness of God. In communities of faith, this is accomplished by giving everyone an opportunity to contribute to the narrative of identity.

- *Ruth shows us that covenant is a commitment to relationship and this commitment embodies God's faithfulness.* In Ruth chapter 1, Ruth forms a covenant with Naomi. The covenant comes out of a dialogue and reframes the construct of identity so that the relationship between Naomi and Ruth holds more sway than the other markers of identity. In other words, the things that would have made Ruth an outsider are overcome by her faithfulness, her *hesed* to her mother-in-law.

- *A commitment to dialogue will require openness to the other and a willingness to see God in new ways.* Faithfulness to dialogue, the commitment to an authentic engagement, demands a level of vulnerability. We reveal ourselves to the other and the other to us. In that exchange, we discover new opportunities to experience God's faithfulness.

Notes

1   "Alzheimer's, Memory and Being," *Speaking of Faith*, American Public Media, Radio Broadcast, March 26, 2009.

2   Regina Schwartz, "Joseph's Bones and the Resurrection of the Text: Remembering in the Bible" in *The Book and the Text: The Bible and Literary Theory*, ed. Regina Schwartz, (Cambridge, MA: Blackwell, 1990), 41.

3   The book of Ruth, along with Song of Songs, Lamentations, Ecclesiastes (Qohelet), and Esther, is one of the five *megillot* or scrolls associated with a festival or observation. Shevu'ot is a festival associated with the harvest, and much of the action in the book takes place at the time of harvest.

4   Kirsten Nielsen, *Ruth*, trans. Edward Broadbridge, Old Testament Library (Louisville: Westminster John Knox, 1997), 94.

No Side, but a Place

Katherine Sonderegger

> The high priests answered Pilate: "We have no king but Caesar." (John 19:15 RSV)

As of old, so today: The high priests speak for us all. We have no king but Caesar. As priests should do, the high priests speak for the people; they give voice to what the whole people of God desire and demand and hope for—and fear. On that day, before the Praetorium, as also now, this priestly task is carried out, fully and solemnly and tragically: They affirm what we stubbornly all believe, we have no king but Caesar.

From the days of Julius Caesar to Germany's modern Kaiser, the great rulers of the earth have styled themselves Caesars, emperors, Roman kings. And like the rulers of our present age, the Roman Caesars and all their courts sought to appeal to the crowds and their leaders, to gain their favor, and to play upon them, upon their desires and fears, as the great instrument of statecraft. Like Elizabeth Tudor, Julius Caesar and all Roman Caesars ruled their lands and nobles and armies, not in spite of, but because they appeared before the crowds: the people of Rome were the Caesar's power.

And like the Caesars, so were the prefects and procurators. Pontius Pilate was no alien to Roman imperial style: he too could play the crowd. Our Evangelist shows us a master at work. Back and forth Pilate goes, from the inner courtyard of his palace to his balcony where he addressed the crowds. Kingship and power, always kingship and power are his main themes. Pilate is a shrewd politician. His power lies with those people, the little satellite nation in the little exotic corner of the empire. He fears them and their power, yes; but he will also conquer them: Our Evangelist shows the chilling efficiency of Pilate's power. He will taunt them with their lack of political power—"Go crucify him yourselves!"—and mock their judgment—"I find no case against him!" He will provoke their threats—" . . . if you do this, you are no friend of Caesar!"—and with a final manipulation of their passion, he presents Christ to them—"Here is your king!"—and wrings from them this final humiliation: "Away with him! We have no king but Caesar." The people of the covenant, the precious possession of God the King, have handed themselves over to Pilate. They have no king on earth but the Roman Caesar (John 19:15, RSV).

As then, so now. As God's own possession, his children called from Jew and Gentile, we cannot believe we have any king but Caesar, and at our shouts of disbelief the lowly King Jesus is handed over and goes his lonely way to the Place of the Skull, his exile outside the city wall.

We have no king but Caesar: Why do we believe this still? Even here, even on the day of Christ's own passion, why do we cling to this lie? Why can we not believe truly—not just with our lips but with our lives—that the gracious Servant of the Lord, Jesus Christ, is King of the world? Perhaps Pilate himself can give us one answer to this haunting question. It is only one, and surely our consciences can supply many, many more. But he does give us one in his exchange with Jesus, deep within the praetorium. "What have you done?" Pilate asks Jesus; he hardly expects a reply. But Jesus gives him this remarkable response: "My kingdom is not of this world. If my kingdom were of this world, my followers would fight to keep me from being handed over. But as it is, my kingdom is not from this side" (John 18:36). Pilate hears from Jesus' lips what we feared all along: This Jesus is not our sort of king. He is not our kind of Caesar at all; he does not even belong to this cosmos, to this age, our age. He has no servants, no guards, no police and inner circle; no one fights for him. The Greek that stands behind our tepid word, *followers*, echoes throughout John's passion: it is the word for the Temple police, for the guards warming themselves by the charcoal fire, for the soldiers who bind Jesus in the garden and lead him away. There is none of this in Jesus' Kingdom, none of this in the exercise of his royal power. There are not even sides to be defended. But it is an unmistakable part of our cosmos, our age, that there *are* sides, and those who fight for them. Our Evangelist shows this in stark physical terms.

There is the garden where Jesus repairs with his disciples set over against the walled city and its powers; there is the outer courtyard with its crowds and priests over against the prefect and his political aims; there is the inner courtyard with the guards and servants and police against Peter; and Peter in his denials against his questioners; Peter against Malchus; Judas against Jesus; and Pilate, moving back and forth, one side to another, meeting fear against fear, threat against threat, power against power. This is the cold-eyed realism of Holy Scripture. It knows our world and paints it with unflinching clarity. To be king in *this* world is to seize a place, defend it, mark it out on all sides, and send your guards and inner circle to fight to keep it safe, to keep it yours. So Caesars have always said, and so we believe. But Jesus is not of this world. He alone, he most of all, is not Caesar. His royal power is not of this world, and he does not have a side—but he does have a place, all the same, in this world.

Jesus Christ is in the *midst* of it. He is in the midst of Pilate's praetorium; in the midst of the Gabbatha, the place of the pavement; he is in the midst of the garden where his betrayer can find and bind him. And most of all, he, King Jesus, is in the midst of bandits and thieves, reigning from the cross placed, scripture tells us, exactly between them, the mediator of us all. These bandits we know: they are the hired hands who climb in and steal the sheep; they are the criminals like Barabbas, released so that Christ may be bound; they are the rebels crucified on Christ's left hand and right; they are the crowds and their high priests, that day and this, who cannot have this lowly king as their Lord. Good Friday is *good* because it is this day, above all others, in which we see and know that though we will not have Christ as our king, he will have us and will rule all the same in our midst. He will stand where we are, when we will not stand with him. He will be lifted up onto his wooden throne in the midst of our cruelty, our polemics, our mockery and betrayal, to be king, our king, precisely there. May this day our eyes be opened to see this king in his royal power; and may all our days be spent in *this* royal courtroom and at *his* side. Amen.

Genesis 22:1–8; Hebrews 10: 1–25; John 18:1–19.37

The Preaching
Congregation,
a Mirror of the Gospel

Judith M. McDaniel

I n the book *God Has a Story Too*, James A. Sanders observes that biblical stories are not models for morality so
much as they are mirrors of identity. In other words, the
stories told in the Bible mirror the identity of God and the
identity of the people whose experience of God resulted in their
telling these stories. The stories of the Bible are a reflection of
God and God's people, and these stories continue to provide a
mirror of character as you and I retell them. They mirror our
character because we have chosen to tell them as stories semi-
nal to our being, and our telling them both mirrors our identity
and changes us. But our telling these stories changes the reflection of God that is portrayed. That is, because our context of
life is different from that of the original storytellers, our telling
of these narratives subtly alters the perception of these stories.
Thereby it could be said that there is an inherent link between
the character of the storyteller or preacher, the character of

the hearers or congregation, and the character of the gospel proclaimed: The three mirror one another.

The grace-filled preacher first listens, watches, gathers, and then gives expression to the dreams for which the congregation has not been able to find words. But in listening before speaking, watching for those places where dreams can flourish, and envisioning together a new reality, the entire worshiping community becomes responsible for proclamation. The entire congregation creates identity and is incarnational. Congregations proclaim and do Christian formation by giving voice to the unique language and practices of the Christian faith. When you and I walk into a nave filled with symbols, proclamation has already started, for symbols communicate. The body language of worshipers communicates. Congregations proclaim by the way they worship, by the way they do adult education, by the way they steward their resources, by the way they take care of their buildings, by the way they do outreach, by the way they live their lives seven days a week. Functioning ministries, ascendant and developing at different times in the life of a parish, move into and out of a center of influence that looks something like this:

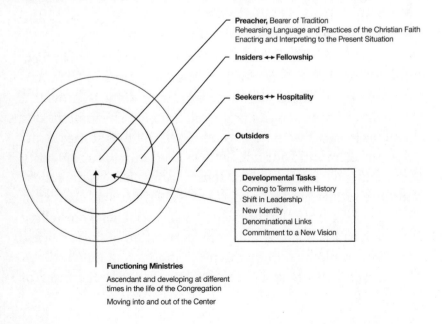

Preacher, Bearer of Tradition
Rehearsing Language and Practices of the Christian Faith
Enacting and Interpreting to the Present Situation

Insiders ←→ Fellowship

Seekers ←→ Hospitality

Outsiders

Developmental Tasks
Coming to Terms with History
Shift in Leadership
New Identity
Denominational Links
Commitment to a New Vision

Functioning Ministries
Ascendant and developing at different times in the life of the Congregation
Moving into and out of the Center

For example, stewardship and Christian education start-up customarily occur in the fall of the year. Thus, those activities move into the center of influence at that time of year. A colleague once described the developmental task of speaking at the center as being for the purpose of creating cognitive dissonance, a void for people to move into. Moving people in this way, he said, is leadership. All the rest is just management. Could it perhaps be added that that void, that space between speaker and people, is a prerequisite for transcendence and transparency?

Individual speakers give voice to the formation being done by the entire community. Gathering, listening, attending to the images, music, and senses, those who speak work with the congregation. The rhythms of the liturgy move individuals and the congregation in and out of moments of leadership in a sequence of events that flows to a climax. One of the things we are striving for is a rhythm that enables us to pray through words of worship, not only focusing on the words, but also using their familiarity to think and pray through them to a deeper reality.

Praying our way through the rhythms of worship brings us into closer contact with the grace of God. Both the habit or routine of worshiping and the movement of the liturgy propel us from the baptismal font to the altar. Similarly, there is a sense of grace in the overall design of liturgy, in its cohesiveness, in its unity. Of course, because of our lectionary, we have a head start on creating a sense of unity. Having a lectionary that sets the tone and mood of our worship experience in readings specific to the rhythm and seasons of the entire church year gives us a sense of wholeness, of movement toward completion. Then from that larger rhythm, we turn to individual services to integrate sermon, music, prayers in such a way as to produce a sense of wholeness and movement within that particular worship experience. However, there are other, more subtle, ways in which the structure of a service invokes a breadth of interpretation while inviting the participation of the entire community of faith in a particular act of worship that is grace-filled.

It would not be too much to say, I think, that in worship we participate in the transformation of the world. I do not mean we go to church to say things and do things that leave the rest of the world outside the church doors. I mean the church in worship acknowledges the real world, the new creation that is coming into being, and we do that in our choice of words, in the act of communication, whether that be the words of music, sermon, scripture, or prayer.

Walter Brueggemann argues in *Finally Comes the Poet*, and I would agree, that "Speech . . . is the central act of communion."[1] By that he means we address and are addressed by the reality of God in speech. Standing at the lectern or in the pulpit, you and I have the power to name God in the world, and out of that naming is evoked a response. "That's a pretty scary responsibility," you may protest; and indeed it is, if we think that for every thing there is a word. But language doesn't work that way. As mentioned earlier, context has an impact on meaning. Words take their meaning from other words.

For example, we all know what the verb "to say" means: The weatherman said it would be cooler today, but he also said it will be warmer tomorrow and that this weather will continue through the weekend. "Said" means reported here, doesn't it? How about she said the issue was clear, she said it was straightforward, she said it was obvious to anyone who really thought about it, she said it was to the point . . . .What does "said" mean here . . . interpreted, hammered a point? Or, you *said* you would do it! You *said* I could count on you! "Said" means promised or made a commitment here, doesn't it? Any one of these definitions of "to say" could be found in the dictionary, but they are all different: report, interpretation, promise. So when we use the word "say," its meaning is not transferred as information from one person to another. It's not as if the thoughts in my head could be delivered to yours as a package. That's a positivist, empiricist, sender-receiver view of communication and reality that is only partially adequate. Words take their meaning from other words. Words themselves are not transparent to their referent. Word meanings are not objective reflections of reality which somehow correspond to the truth as if representative containers of it. Communication, and communion, are more complicated than that.

"A word fitly spoken is like apples of gold in pictures of silver" wrote the author of Proverbs 25:11. The translation I just read is from the King James Version of the Bible. The NRSV renders Proverbs 25:11—"A word fitly spoken is like apples of gold in a setting of silver." "A word fitly spoken" refers to diction in both its meanings: first, the choice of words and, second, the enunciation or delivery of those words. The words we choose to interpret a text, like Paul's choosing the words of his letters, create theology as we compose our sermons. But even in the second meaning of diction, the enunciation or delivery of the words of scripture, we are involved in interpretation, for there is no such thing as reading aloud without interpretation. Reading scripture in a flat monotone is an interpretation of that scripture. And what does a flat, monotone interpretation convey? Lifelessness, disbelief, the absence of God.

On the other hand, oral interpretation is not synonymous with performance. I am chary about the use of the word "performance" in relation to anything done in church. I always tell my chapel team on their first, nervous morning of leading worship for the seminary community that nothing can go wrong because what we're about to do is *not* a performance. It is a worship service. To many people "performance" means a presentation, like putting on a show. I prefer to speak of what we do in worship as a rehearsal of the language and practices of the Christian faith, an enactment that makes present or effects what we're speaking aloud.

To effect or make happen by our words is what is called "Speech-Acts Theory." For example, baptism is effected by water and word. When the priest says, "I baptize you in the name of the Father, and of the Son, and of the Holy Spirit," she is effecting baptism. Her words, together with water, are making baptism happen. Or when the priest says, "Now that he and she have given themselves to each other by solemn vows, with the joining of hands and the giving and receiving of rings, I pronounce that they are husband and wife . . . ," her words are bringing into being a new reality. A word fitly spoken is not only a moment of beauty like apples of gold in pictures of silver. A word aptly spoken is a moment of grace.

So we take the rhythms of the liturgy seriously. The words of the liturgy are not yours or mine to alter at will, for the liturgy belongs to all the faithful, who have a right to know what words they will use in worship. Liturgy is the rehearsal of the voice of the Church, the work of the people. Oral interpretation is a spiritual practice, not a method.

When you and I lift our voices in songs of praise or stand at the lectern or pulpit or around the table, we present a portion of past Christian history and a proclamation of good news for the present that connects a word from the past with the perceptions of the present. If we are effective, we act as enablers and participants in that connection between what is known or called to memory with what all of us are groping to know. As we enter into dialogical relationship with the biblical text to constitute a world rather than represent one long past, we move toward meaning, and it is in that movement toward meaning that a new experience and, thereby, a new reality is expressed. In conversation with the text and in the conversation between lectern and pew, we recognize a semantic space wherein the possibility of a new creation resides. Standing on the horizon of this new creation, the speaker's understanding is relational, dialogical, and interpersonal. The speaker knows he or she is tradition-, language-, and culture-bound but with that knowledge is ready to proclaim a message that is open to creative, mutual sense-making. And in that new creation that lies between partners in theological conversation where perceptions mingle, realities emerge and meanings awaken, there resides the potential for holiness.

You and I know from experience that congregations do have character. But a congregation's character or ethos can become so distinctive that it ceases to be open to being converted. When a congregation and its leadership become entrenched in one style or category of identity, they risk losing the capacity for the growth which the gospel demands. Put another way, a preacher and a congregation who refuse to change make a category mistake.

A category mistake is a term taken from logic. For example, you are seated in a restaurant and the waiter refills your water glass without your having to ask. "Thank you," you say. "No problem," replies the waiter. You weren't talking about problems. You haven't even raised the fact that the water level in your glass is down an inch or so. You are simply responding to an act of attention on the part of the waiter. You are expressing gratitude. But instead of replying "You're welcome," the waiter changes the tenor of the conversation from thanksgiving to difficulty. You and the waiter are holding a conversation, but each is participating in an exchange of a different character, an unconscious category mistake. In this case, the category mistake is less a failure to understand than simply a flawed idiomatic habit.

Then consider televised political debates: The moderator asks a question, and instead of answering the question, the candidate shifts his answer into something *he* wants to talk about. Without acknowledging failure, the moderator then asks the same question of the other candidate, and the identical thing happens: The candidate shifts into another venue. Thus the debate continues . . . in category-mistake mode, with candidates talking past each other, all the while eluding the moderator. In this case, the candidates fully understand the issue and purposely choose not to answer, a conscious category mistake.

But category mistakes happen in conversation when we aren't consciously failing to answer. Category mistakes happen when we are trying to respond in kind. We talk past each other, failing to communicate, when we do not listen fully and fail to comprehend. In the Gospel according to John, for example, Jesus says to the woman who has come to draw water from the well, "If you had asked, I would have given you living water." And the woman responds, "You don't even have a bucket" (John 4:11, *The Message*), a category mistake of life-altering proportions.

Or take the lack of logic in another story of baptism, the story of the man born blind as told in the Gospel of John (9:1–38). In this story the category mistakes are both conscious and unconscious, both purposeful and uncomprehending. Here is the narrative of a worshiper who moves from the ordinary to the extra-ordinary, from coping with the absence of God to living in God's presence, from blindness to sight. For here is a man who has been brought up in the synagogue, whose parents are faithful worshipers in the synagogue, for whom being a part of the Jewish faith defines his place in the community. Here is a man for whom categories of worship change. Here is a man whose value system is altered from intellectual to experiential, who is wrested from physical event to spiritual communion. And it is no joy ride.

Jesus' own disciples make the first category mistake: "Who sinned?" they ask, "This man or his parents, that he was born blind?" The question of sin, who is "in" and who is "out," permeates the scene. First, physical affliction is categorized as a sign of sinfulness, a category mistake of major proportions. It isn't just that it's a mistake to assign people to categories, characterizing them as sinful or unworthy or unable. The point is that there are ways of thinking that are category mistakes. Jesus demonstrates what a mistake such categorization is. He reaches out to the man born blind and then disappears from the scene, leaving the man to follow his instructions. Immediately the man acts. He goes to the pool of Siloam, washes, and sees! But then his troubles begin. He tries to go home, but no joy, celebration, or welcome greet him, only questions and doubts. "Who are you?" his neighbors ask. "Who is this Jesus?" He has no answer, so his neighbors haul him up before the Pharisees.

Scene two: "Are you sure you can see? Were you really blind? Who did it? On the Sabbath! Anathema!" The one who takes action to relieve the affliction is likewise categorized by others as sinful.

You and I may have a little trouble understanding this particular complaint from the Pharisees. We've moved from calling the principal day of worship the "Sabbath" to . . . the Lord's Day to . . . Sunday to . . . the weekend. We have very little experience of the importance of the Sabbath to those first-century worshipers. For them nothing takes precedence over the Sabbath, but also nothing but worship is to be accomplished on this day. So how could someone who violates the Sabbath perform miracles? They cannot believe he is a prophet, another category mistake.

Thus, scene three: They call in the man's parents. Here indeed is a pitiful prospect. Whatever joy his parents might feel at his healing is now overcome by fear. Expulsion from the synagogue and social disgrace are a high price to pay for having a son specially blessed by God. This price they are unwilling to pay. Their mistake comes from different motivation than that of the Pharisees, but it is just as purposeful and just as uncomprehending.

As the drama approaches its climax, we are tempted to ask, "Where has Jesus gone? Why is this man being hounded? He is a good Jew. He has never asked to be healed, so why isn't he getting some kind of support? Where is God?" Perhaps no biblical story illustrates quite so dramatically the truth of our own experience: God's favor more often leads into than away from immediate difficulties. A relationship with God does not remove one *from* but often places one *in* the line of fire. Those who preach faith as the cessation of pain, suffering, poverty, restless nights and turbulent days are offering false comfort. For the worst is about to happen to this man: He is going to be denounced, along with Jesus, and expelled from his community as a sinner. He will no longer be welcome at his old place of worship. He will no longer be part of the kinship that gives him identity. He will be a human without a place. His entire character will be a category mistake.

From Roman catacomb frescoes of the second century, records of pilgrimage to Jerusalem in the fourth century, and

Milanese, Syrian, Jacobite, and Greek liturgies, we know that the earliest Christians understood this gospel to bear witness to baptism and the meaning of Christian initiation. In line with ancient tradition in preparation for baptisms at the Easter Vigil, we read on consecutive Sundays in Lent of year "A" the conversion of the woman at the well together with the story of the blind man whose sight is restored in the Pool of Siloam and then the raising of Lazarus from the dead. We will understand all three stories to hold up before us Christian formation and change from one category of character to another. Focusing on the blind man's story of formation, we recognize the transformation of individual character, but we also cannot avoid acknowledging that the worshiping community has character as well. The author of the gospel according to John has placed in this passage a prominent symbol, a Greek word, αποσυναγαγος (*aposunagagos*), meaning "out of the synagogue" (9:22), a signal of significance found in only two other places (12:42; 16:2) in this gospel. Here we are reminded that the character of the first Christians was Hebrew, and they wanted to remain so. They wanted to continue worshiping in the synagogue, simply adding to their adoration of God their new understanding in the light of Christ. But the community of worship in which they lived and moved and had their being would not let them give voice to their new understanding. "Stay in character," preached the synagogue community, "or we will cast you out." And cast out they were.

Just as surely as synagogue congregations had character then, each church congregation has character and personality of its own today. Congregations make category mistakes: They forget what their character is. They forget that their character is to reach for something more. How that character is communicated is the responsibility of the entire worshiping community. Congregations preach. "Preaching is not . . . one person's persuasive address. It is the ceaseless activity of the church,"[2] according to Rick Lischer, professor of homiletics at Duke. Sometimes category mistakes happen. Sometimes congregations lose sight and understanding. A system responds to its lowest level, so a congregation must constantly ask itself, "What character am I communicating? Am I simply mirroring the categories of the culture surrounding me? Am I preaching self-satisfaction because I am unwilling to disturb the comfort level I have attained? Or am I reaching beyond myself to new life?"

A man born blind has his eyes opened and his whole character changes. That change costs him dearly, and it is grace. That change is grace because with each obstacle, he grows in faith. That change is grace because as he meets each challenge, he becomes more open to the light. That change is grace because it makes of him a witness. And that change is grace because it is then that Jesus returns.

We have said that at least part of the iconic nature of retelling the biblical story is its capacity both to change and to create identity. We have reflected on a change of character, but in what way does retelling the story create identity? What does creating identity mean? In part it means that in reading the Bible, we are vulnerable to its capacity to author identity and values in those who listen to its words, creating the capacity for understanding and acting in new ways as God's people. In the preacher's mouth the words of the Bible with their capacity to author become the preacher's "authority." The preacher speaks and says, "This is what I see," in such a way as to ask, either explicitly or implicitly, "What do you see?" People often don't grasp their own identity until they voice those things most important to them, don't know their practices until they say them out loud, participate in them, and view them from different angles.

This is what I see. What do you see? Or put another way, what do you seek? "What do you seek?" are the first words of Jesus recorded in the Gospel according to John, the first words of significance, the first spoken to his disciples (John 1:38, NASB). "What do you seek?" will echo again and again; for over and over people will come to him, searching.

It has been said that the religious person believes life is about taking some kind of journey. The non-religious person believes there is no journey to take. Many people had come to John in those days to immerse themselves in the river Jordan and be baptized in his presence. They were a motley collection, but they had one thing in common: Like us, they were on a journey, searching for some answers to the meaning of life, searching for God, searching for the meaning of our relationships to one another, the meaning of one's own existence. Yes, they, like we, were searching.

John preached a baptism of repentance in order to receive forgiveness of sins, in order to be made acceptable. John preached also that new life was coming, coming in the future. But unlike John and his contemporaries, we seem to have lost faith in the future. We are not seeking simply release from the evils that pursue us. We are seeking solutions. We are seeking our heart's deepest desires, now. And yet as Jesus asks of us, "What do you seek?" the question initiates a terrible longing. His question strips away our lesser goals and threatens our hard-won understanding, for we recognize that that for which we yearn we have not imagined.

"I've heard these passages read year after year in church," we say to ourselves, "and nothing has really changed. There were no apostles in the Fourth Gospel and there aren't any now, just disciples, learners, and we don't seem to be getting any smarter. Sure, something special happened two thousand years ago, but that long ago event is just that—long, long ago—and what I see around me now is not encouraging: We're done with the Cold War and back to hot ones. We've got more work than we can do, bills than we can pay, taxes than we can manage; and as we get older, more illness and death than we can deal with. Life is so . . . *daily*. It's hard to believe there could be something to seek that we haven't tried before."

Yes, it is easy to become discouraged with the tedium, weariness, and out-and-out pain of living. And we're in good company: Certainly Isaiah is discouraged when he says in the Old

Testament, "I have labored in vain, I have spent my strength for nothing" (Isaiah 49:4). John and even Jesus knew discouragement in their lives.

But their struggles seem somehow more stirring than ours. They confronted the wrath of kings. Our struggles are more mechanical: "How am I ever going to make it to payday?" Their victories were glorious. Ours are ordinary: "I finally got Visa paid off; now I can tackle MasterCard." When it comes to witnessing to the faith, their words were immortalized, while you and I are often met with indifference when we try to tell people we are Christians. Their vision of God was clear. And we confuse anamnesis with nostalgia. Discouraged? We're not only discouraged, we're on the verge of accepting something far less than that for which we seek.

Somewhere in the past you and I have come to our own river Jordan. We have been baptized, washed in the blood of the lamb, and made acceptable to God, but we remain unchanged, unconverted. We do not expect to *see* the reality of God in our everyday, mundane lives. And such lack of expectation is a self-fulfilling prophecy; for expecting nothing, we see nothing.

Are you and I unconverted because the promises we made or our parents made for us at our baptism weren't real? Was there so little at stake that it didn't matter what we promised? No. There was everything at stake, and somehow we knew so.

Do we remain unconverted because we expected baptism to be some sort of magical cure-all that would change all the bad guys to good guys and smooth out all the rough places that appear in everyone's path over the years? There may have been a little of that illusion.

Or are we among the unconverted baptized because we have not acknowledged the undeserved, unearned favor of God? Unconverted because we have chosen instead to rely on ourselves rather than put our trust in the Christ, to seek his face in each day that is given us. We seek transformation, but our lives are so cluttered with concern that we can make no space for the grace of God. Then it is no wonder we witness to tedium, for our stories contain too much of us and too little of him whose life sustains us.

"I am interested in the people who made the Bible, but I am more interested in the people whom the Bible makes, for they show me the fibre and genius of Scripture as no mental studiousness or verbal exegesis can do," wrote Charles Henry Parkhurst.[3] Whether as individuals or as members of a congregation, the people whom the Bible makes preach. As they mirror the character of the gospel, they ask, "What do you seek?" They are the words asked of adult catechumens seeking baptism and Jesus' first words to his disciples. "Whom do you seek?" They are his words asked of the arresting soldiers at his betrayal, and asked again of Mary Magdalene outside the tomb. "What do you seek?" They are the words asked of you and me everyday. What is the identity you and I see when we look in the mirror? Whether our actions are quiet or assertive, measured or forthright, we are all the same: We are the baptized whose identity mirrors a vision larger than ourselves. "What do you seek?" he asks. We have only to respond, "New life in Christ," and he will reply, "Come . . . and see."

Notes

1 Walter Brueggemann, *Finally Comes the Poet* (Minneapolis: Fortress Press, 1989), 44.

2 Richard Lischer, in Thomas G. Long, ed., *Listening to the Word: Studies in Honor of Fred B. Craddock* (Nashville: Abingdon Press, 1993), 128.

3 Quoted in Thomas Harwood Pattison, *The History of the English Bible* (Philadelphia: American Baptist Publication Society, 1894), 222.

The Love of *Lernen* and the Desire for God: On Seminary Training and Its Afterlife

Roger Ferlo

I was once the rector of a small academic parish situated in the middle of a large and thriving Jewish neighborhood in Pittsburgh, Pennsylvania. My church building sat on Forbes Avenue cheek by jowl with the largest Jewish Community Center this side of Tel Aviv. There were sixteen synagogues in that neighborhood, some of them affluent and influential, some of them just storefronts, a few just occupying a room or two in the rented house of a Russian immigrant. There was also a long-established Catholic parish in the neighborhood, along with the *Sixth* Presbyterian Church (this was Calvinist southwest Pennsylvania, after all), a Swedenborgian meeting house, and, in the shadow of the Jewish Community Center, our own little Church of the Redeemer.

Just a few blocks up the street from the Redeemer rectory a group of Hasidic families had demarcated the invisible lines that bounded the territory around their *shul.* They had strung up an *evruv*—an inconspicuous, all but invisible network of wires that linked and enclosed several city blocks. In a Hasidic neighborhood, you set off an *evruv* in order to create a safe ritual space where some laws of Sabbath keeping could be suspended, a designated block or two where you could push strollers full of kids on Saturday morning, or arrange to pick up your groceries. By stringing up an *evruv,* the local Hasidim had created a kind of virtual village—a *shtetl*— in the midst of rust-belt America.

One brilliant Saturday morning, a clergy colleague of mine was entertaining her elderly mother, an elegant, proper Protestant lady of a certain age who was visiting from California. My friend needed to drive her mother through the Hasidic neighborhood in order to get to an appointment in another part of town. As usual on a Sabbath morning, there were large groups of Hasidic families walking toward the synagogue. The women were dressed beautifully but soberly, with longish skirts and sensible shoes, their heads covered by a scarf or snood; the men and boys were dressed in black suits and white shirts, and were wearing their distinctive broad-brimmed black hats. My friend's mother watched the proceedings with evident interest as they drove through the neighborhood. After much thought, she then turned to her daughter and remarked: "I had no idea there were so many Amish people living here in Pittsburgh."

I learned a lot from my Jewish friends and colleagues in that neighborhood, as different as their religious lives were from mine. I learned about honest friendship, about the power of ideas and the murderous danger of ideology, about how the way of Torah was the way of life. Perhaps the greatest compliment I have ever been paid came from a rabbi I had just befriended. We had spent a pleasant afternoon talking about the ways that our scriptures and our traditions had shaped our lives. As he left he said "Thanks for this time together—it would be good for us to get together again for some *lernen* some time soon."

To translate the Yiddish word *lernen* simply as "learning" doesn't quite capture its semantic resonance. For a true lover of Torah, *lernen* is not about schooling; it's about a way of life, an approach to scripture that discerns the power of the Spirit in the all-too-human give-and-take of honest conversation grounded in the sacred text. It is a recognition that divine truth is revealed most plainly only in community and in relationship—in the communities we form around the sacred page, in the honest relationships which such community creates and fosters. Scripture reading is never a private affair. Authentic scripture readers are contradictory, argumentative, not necessarily in agreement, but united in reverence for a sacred text inspired by God, a text that itself speaks in many voices. And just as importantly, such authentic readers are also united in loving respect for each other, despite their deepest differences. To engage scripture in this way is to create communities of readers who take a deep joy both in the text and in each other's company, who in this ancient work of *lernen* experience a new lightness of being, as the Spirit of God lifts the conversation to the things of life that really matter. I have always thought that it was this kind of sheer delight in the act of reading that shaped and nurtured Jesus' own revolutionary understanding of Torah. And when we are true to ourselves and to our calling, it is that sheer delight in the act of reading that shapes and nurtures those who teach and those who learn in our theological schools.

"I opened my mouth, and said, acquire wisdom for yourselves without money; Put your neck under her yoke, and let your souls receive instruction, it is to be found close by" (Sirach 51:25–26). One of the lovely paradoxes of *lernen* is the odd way that the Wisdom tradition, and the rabbis and teachers who followed Wisdom, both in Jesus' day and later, characterized this discipline of Torah reading. Put your neck under her yoke, says the book of the Wisdom of ben Sirach. "Take upon yourself the yoke of the Kingdom of Heaven," says the *Mishnah*.[1] Recite the

Shema at dawn—that the Lord our God is one God—because your first act of daily life is to take the yoke of the Kingdom upon you. *Torah ora*: the Law is our Light!

Knowing this, and knowing that as a Jew Jesus knew this, and that Matthew knew that Jesus knew this, one realizes the power of Matthew's polemic against the Pharisees, who in his mind have weighted down this joyful yoke with the heavy burden of rule and scruple. "Come unto me," says Matthew's Jesus, "come unto me all you who are weary and are carrying heavy burdens, and I will give you rest. Take my yoke upon you, and learn from me; for I am gentle and humble in heart, and you will find rest for your souls. For *my* yoke is easy, and *my* burden is light" (Matthew 11:28–30). In a way, these sayings of Jesus allowed Matthew in writing this gospel to call together a new community of *lernen*, one that every successive Christian reader of scripture is invited to share. In this time of division in the Anglican Communion, and among our own Episcopal churches, it is good to be reminded of this Matthean energy. The joy of the Torah finds its renewal not in the closed circles of the rule-bound and proof-texting sectarian and schismatic mind, but in the incarnation and restoration of Wisdom herself, in the very person of Jesus.

"Take my yoke upon you, and learn from me." One must walk this way with caution. This is risky ground. This same Jesus whose yoke is so much easier than the yoke of the Pharisees is also the troubling and troublesome teacher who admonishes his followers to leave everything behind and to take up the heavy yoke of the cross. To deepen the paradox even more, the very heaviness of that yoke, borne by Christ alone, has against all reason and expectation restored the lightness and delight of Torah joy in the believing reader, unlocking and revealing to us in the Word of scripture the very Word made flesh. In cross and resurrection, in the power of the Holy Spirit blowing through our midst, Christ is made alive and vibrant in us, here, now, as readers and hearers and doers of the Word, in the continuing discipline of holy reading and holy living—in the lively, contradictory, polemical, dialectical, open and open-ended community of *lernen*—to which every Christian is called, a yoke which following Matthew's example Christians now joyously assume as our own.

One of the things I liked about living in Pittsburgh so close to that Hasidic neighborhood was how matters secular and matters religious were at once so separate from each other and always so intermixed, especially in the rough and tumble of urban life. You can say the same for the mixed-up ritual we engage in when we gather for graduation at a theological school. It's a secular ceremony with religious roots, a religious ceremony with secular implications. One sits in what could pass for a high-school auditorium and behaves as if it were a church— proclaiming churchly things in the context of a secular ritual. On such occasions, we listen to a commencement address as if it were a sermon. Or do we listen to a sermon as if it were a commencement address? And to make matters even more confusing, we clothe our graduates with a secular symbol of intellectual accomplishment—an academic hood—that also symbolizes the very different kind of yoke that the rabbis and Matthew and Jesus talked about and celebrated.

This association is what makes seminary education so distinctive. Scholarly appurtenances like academic hoods function not simply as the secular symbols of advanced degrees, but also as symbols of the yoke of the Kingdom of Heaven, the outward and visible signs of our shared commitment to the way of the Torah that is the way of Christ, a commitment to the act of *lernen* that my rabbi friend cherished so deeply, a commitment to the act of loving the Lord our God with all our minds as well as with all our hearts, and loving our neighbors as ourselves. Our graduates receive their flimsy hoods as signs of a lifelong commitment to the life of the mind in service to the life of the soul, and not just their own minds and souls, but also the minds and souls of all whom they encounter as teachers, pastors, administrators, counselors. In a time of deep doctrinal and moral disagreement, it is essential that faculty and students alike embrace the gentleness and humbleness of heart that are essential to the ministry of teaching and learning to which they have been called.

There is a dangerous contradiction haunting our hallowed rituals. It is the danger of spiritual pride and intellectual hubris, the conviction that our educational achievements have somehow set us apart, that in earning our degrees we have been inducted into some kind of intellectual elite. Of course, such arrogance flies in the face of what the gospel insists upon when it comes to knowledge. As Paul might have said, the more we know about the things of God, the more we know how little we know. Or as Jesus says in Matthew's gospel, "I thank you, Father, Lord of heaven and earth, because you have hidden these things from the wise and intelligent and have revealed them to infants" (Matthew 11:25). When those of us who wear these academic hoods, who bear these academic yokes, are honest with ourselves, we know that our knowledge of God and the ways of God is all-too-partial, all-too-human. We long ago entered the great cloud of unknowing. As Paul once famously remarked to all those smart people in Corinth: "Look around you. What do you see? Where is the one who is wise?"

But there's also another danger, a danger faced by everyone who plans to enter the ordained life. It is not so much the danger of pride (although no one in a theological school is immune from that particular failing). It is the danger of intellectual and spiritual complacency, of intellectual and spiritual laziness, grounded in the perhaps understandable conviction that once an aspiring ordinand has run through the seminary curriculum—once she has fulfilled all righteousness, once she has dotted every "*shin*" and crossed every "*tau*" in every last exam, once she has hurdled every hurdle that a commission on ministry or a board of examining chaplains or a senior thesis advisor has placed in her path—then enough is enough, and from here on out all she needs to know is Jesus. In our parishes and in the wider church she will encounter many people who will tell her this, especially when she seeks to take some Sabbath time to read, to learn, to reconsider, and to cultivate the seeds that have been planted in her three years of seminary training.

There are all too many experiences in the ordained life of the American Church where a deep resistance to learning will make itself felt. It can be felt in a popular culture increasingly hostile to the educated mind. It can be felt in a political culture where strident voices pillory knowledge and expertise as somehow undemocratic and elitist. It can be felt in a religious culture where the give-and-take of the intellectual life is perceived as an alien threat to people of faith. Those entering the ordained life must steadily resist such know-nothing religion. They must wear the yoke of their continuing learning with passion and determination, and so demonstrate to their parishioners and to the larger world that the love of learning and the desire for God are one and the same love, and a life-long enterprise—an enterprise that as teacher and pastor and priest our graduates seek to share with those they serve.

In keeping with my Hasidic theme, it is tempting to end this meditation with the praise of Torah found in the *Zohar*, that wonderfully bizarre fourteenth-century compendium of Jewish mystical texts. The author imagines the Torah as a beautiful and attractive woman (like Wisdom herself in the tradition) "disclosing her innermost secrets only to those who love her."[2] The kabbalistic imagination gets a little erotic and steamy at this point, so it might be safer to end on a slightly less sexist note, with a text dating from the same period, but landing perhaps a bit closer to home. It is late in Dante's *Purgatorio*. The shade of Vergil is taking his leave of Dante the pilgrim, whom he has guided through all the circles of hell, and now almost to the top of the seven-story purgatorial mountain. The have braved and endured the circles of pride and anger, wrath and sloth—qualities Dante recognized as all too familiar in himself, as they are all too familiar in the lives of academics, bishops, and priests. But Dante's purgatory is not about punishment. It is about conversion of life. Counter to all the theological assumptions of his day, Dante doesn't imagine purgatory as a vengeful cauldron of fire filled with suffering souls. Dante re-imagines purgatory as a vast theme-park of conversion, a magic mountain of repentance, full of poets and artists and musicians and princes and scholars, with the earthly paradise itself accessible to the redeemed and chastened soul that has reached the mountain's peak. As an unbelieving pagan, Vergil knows that he cannot himself cross into the sacred precincts of a restored Eden. His time as teacher, counselor and mentor is drawing to a close:

> . . . The temporal fire and the eternal
> You have seen, my son, and now come to a place
> In which, unaided, I can see no farther.
>
> I have brought you here with intellect and skill.
> From now on take your pleasure as your guide.
> You are free of the steep way, and free of the narrow.
>
> Look at the sun shining before you,
> Look at the fresh grasses, flowers and trees
> Which here the earth produces of itself.

> No longer wait for word or sign from me.
> Your will is free, upright and sound.
> Not to act as it chooses is unworthy:
> Over yourself I crown and miter you.[3]

As valedictories go, that's about as good as it gets. We cannot promise our graduates what Vergil promised Dante, entry into any sort of earthly paradise. No one engaged in seminary education harbors any illusions about the church on that score. Nor, thank God, can we offer them crown and miter (who would wish either on anyone in these parlous times?). Those flimsy academic hoods must suffice: poor things, but our own. As teachers and scholars, we can only offer our students what has been offered to us—the reward of lives marked, like Dante's own, by a deep love of learning fired by a burning desire for God.

Notes

1   Claude Joseph Goldsmid Montefiore and Herbert Martin James Loewe, *A Rabbinic Anthology* (New York, Schocken Books, 1974), 200.

2   Gershom Scholem, ed., *Zohar the Book of Splendor* (New York: Schocken Books, 1963), 89.

3   Dante Alighieri, *Purgatorio*, xxvii, 127–42; Hollander translation.

Afterword

In 1943, Alexander C. Zabriskie edited a volume of essays in honor of his predecessor as dean—the Rev. Dr. Wallace Eugene Rollins. It is an intriguing set of essays collected around the title *Anglican Evangelicalism*. The book divides into three sections: "historical," "constructive theology," and the "practical application of evangelical principles." In these three sections, an argument slowly emerges. It is an argument that calls for a "thinking evangelicalism," which is deeply committed to mission and to pastoral and social life. So on the "thinking" end of the spectrum, we find Stanley Brown-Serman's essay on the Bible. He sees the emergence of a new evangelicalism which "stresses God's activity within history, and the culmination of God's revelation in the life, person, and work of Jesus, whose historical character and place in human history must not be forgotten."[1] So in contrast with the "older evangelicals," who tended to see the life of Jesus as a prelude to the work of atonement on the cross, Brown-Serman is calling for a deeper recognition of the work of revelation that occurs in the life. In short, for Brown-Serman, the life of Jesus matters as much as the death of Jesus. The theme of mission is explicitly confronted in several essays. It also appears in places that one would not expect it to be addressed. So, for example, there is a strong apologetic feel to the essay by Charles Wesley Lowry on "the situation and need of man[kind]." Lowry argues that a Christian view of humanity is much more powerful and accurate than the view of humanity emerging from liberalism, fascism, and communism. The commitment to the pastoral and social dimension of the gospel is best captured by Albert Mollegen's essay. Mollegen is opposed to explicit participation in politics by the church, but constantly calls on the church to encourage faithful witness and participation as members of civic society. These essays are set in a certain time; the political and social situation in Europe hovers in the background. They are a thoughtful engagement with the challenge of the Seminary to be faithful to the past, yet open to the future.

As I read these essays in this book by my distinguished colleagues, it is striking how the same spirit is present in the text. Our challenge as a seminary is to live with difference. We disagree about important questions. And the question is: how far can disagreement extend in a seminary community?

These essays provide a multifaceted answer. First, there is a shared approach that stresses the centrality of the biblical witness in our life together. Much like the volume edited by Zabriskie, the Bible is not only explicitly discussed by A. Katherine Grieb, Stephen Cook, John Yieh, and Judy Fentress Williams, but is also figuring prominently in essays on mission and "opening the table." Herein is an important witness: we live with differences around a shared core. This shared core is the affirmation that God has spoken. God's Eternal Word has been made manifest and we learn from the Eternal Word through the written Word.

Second, these essays invite colleagues to make a case. A good illustration of this is Stephen Edmondson's thoughtful argument for "opening the table." Although there are those in the Seminary community who believe that this is misguided in both theology and practice, there is a recognition that we need to listen to the case well made. The Church has an obligation to discern with humility what the Spirit is teaching us. Part of the hard work of discernment is listening to the conversation. Although I am not persuaded by Edmondson's argument, I appreciate the voice and seek to honor that voice in the conversation.

Third, these essays recognize the continuing importance of mission. We must never allow the preoccupation with conversation internally to neglect the importance of witness. Several essays make the case for reaching out and beyond. Our editors—Richard Jones and Barney Hawkins—make the case in a compelling way. We must remain a seminary that seeks to serve and bring the "good news" to this world of pain and hurt.

The spirit that pervades these essays is one that my predecessor Dean Martha Horne modeled. The vast majority of the contributors were appointed by Dean Horne. She ensured that Virginia Theological Seminary remained a community rooted in the witness of scripture, yet open to the conversation and the leading of the Holy Spirit. Dean Horne was a remarkable leader of this Seminary community. She understood the challenges of the time. She also understood the need for the Seminary to be in deep continuity with the past. In the foreword to the Zabriskie volume, Presiding Bishop Henry St. George Tucker wrote of Dr. Rollins:

> He is a man whose own deep personal convictions do not preclude his recognition of values inherent in other points of view. His attitude towards these others was not simply one of politeness towards possibilities. He showed that a true Evangelical is also a true Catholic, for he is one who rejoices that in Christ Jesus many differing points of view have been brought together into a real unity.[2]

These sentiments were not simply true of the leadership under Dr. Rollins, but are also true of the leadership under Dean Horne. We honor her witness, service, and love for the Seminary, and we are grateful for the spirit of conversation and living with difference which she modeled and made possible.

The Very Rev. Ian Markham
Dean and President

Notes

1   Stanley Brown-Serman, "The Evangelicals and the Bible," in *Anglican Evangelicalism*, ed. Alexander Zabriskie (Philadelphia: The Church Historical Society 1943), 100.

2   Henry St. George Tucker, "Foreword" in *Anglican Evangelicalism*, ed. Alexander Zabriskie (Philadelphia: The Church Historical Society 1943), xiv.

List of Contributors

Mitzi J. Budde, D.Min, is Head Librarian and Professor at Virginia Theological Seminary, Alexandria, VA.

Stephen L. Cook, Ph.D. is the Catherine N. McBurney Professor of Old Testament Language and Literature at Virginia Theological Seminary, Alexandria, VA.

The Rev. Stephen B. Edmondson, Ph.D., currently serves as the rector of St. Thomas Episcopal Church in McLean, Virginia, and is a former Associate Professor of Church History at the Virginia Theological Seminary, Alexandria, VA.

Judy Fentress-Williams, Ph.D. is Associate Professor of Old Testament at Virginia Theological Seminary, Alexandria, VA.

The Rev. Roger A. Ferlo, Ph.D. is Associate Dean and Director of the Institute for Christian Formation and Leadership, and Professor of Religion and Culture at Virginia Theological Seminary, Alexandria, VA.

The Rev. A. Katherine Grieb, Ph.D. is Professor of New Testament at Virginia Theological Seminary, Alexandria, VA.

The Rev. J. Barney Hawkins IV, Ph.D. is the Vice-President for Institutional Advancement, Associate Dean for the Center for Anglican Communion Studies and Professor of Pastoral Theology at Virginia Theological Seminary, Alexandria, VA.

The Rev. Richard J. Jones, Ph.D., Professor Emeritus of Mission and World Religions at Virginia Theological Seminary, Alexandria, VA.

The Rt. Rev. Peter James Lee, is serving as Interim Dean of Grace Cathedral in San Francisco. Bishop Lee previously served as Bishop of Virginia from 1985–2009 and chaired the Virginia Theological Seminary Board of Trustees from 1993–2009.

The Very Rev. Ian S. Markham, Ph.D. is the Dean and President, and Professor of Theology and Ethics at Virginia Theological Seminary, Alexandria, VA.

The Rev. Judith M. McDaniel, Ph.D. is the Howard Chandler Robbins Professor of Homiletics at Virginia Theological Seminary, Alexandria, VA.

Allan M. Parrent, Ph.D., Associate Dean for Academic Affairs and Vice President, 1983–1997, Member of the Virginia Theological Seminary faculty from 1972–1997, and the Clinton S. Quin Professor Emeritus of Christian Ethics at Virginia Theological Seminary, Alexandria, VA.

The Rev. Robert W. Prichard, Ph.D. is the Arthur Lee Kinsolving Professor of Christianity in America and Instructor in Liturgy at Virginia Theological Seminary, Alexandria, VA.

Timothy F. Sedgwick, Ph.D. is Vice President and Associate Dean of Academic Affairs, and the Clinton S. Quin Professor of Christian Ethics at Virginia Theological Seminary, Alexandria, VA.

The Rev. Katherine Sonderegger, Ph.D. is Professor of Theology at Virginia Theological Seminary, Alexandria, VA.

The Rev. John Yueh-Han Yieh, Ph.D. is Professor of New Testament at Virginia Theological Seminary, Alexandria, VA.